The BHS First Pony Manual

The British Horse Society

A guide for parents and first-time owners

DEBBY FROWEN AND MADELEINE RIDGE BHSISM

EDITED BY JO WINFIELD FBHS

J.A. ALLEN · LONDON

First published in Great Britain in 2014 by

J.A. Allen
Clerkenwell House
Clerkenwell Green
London EC1R OHT

J.A. Allen is an imprint of Robert Hale Limited
www.allenbooks.co.uk

ISBN 978-1-908809-15-5

British Library Cataloguing in Publication Data
A catalogue record for this book is available from the British Library

Designed and typeset by Paul Saunders
Printed in China by 1010 Printing International Ltd

Disclaimer of Liability

The authors and publisher shall have neither liability nor responsibility to
any person or entity with respect to any loss or damage caused or alleged to
be caused directly or indirectly by the information contained in this book.
While the book is as accurate as the authors can make it, there may be errors,
omissions and inaccuracies.

It is recommended that, whenever riding and whilst dealing with
behavioural problems in horse and ponies, a hard hat approved to
current standards be worn.

Contents

Acknowledgements

The authors would like to thank the following individuals for their help in setting up the photo shoots:

Ella Frowen, Clare Blunsden, Isobel Mills, Megan Wheatley, Georgina McMichael, Jonathan Keen, Alison Crook of Stroud Saddlery, Jo Charles, Sarah Bevan, Watershed RDA, and Stella Drury.

Photographs and illustrations

All photos are by Charlotte Bellamy, except for the following:

Those on pages 18, 64, 65, 78, 97, 127, 137, 140, 141, 142, 143, 145, 156, 157 by Event-Digipix

Those on pages 37, 39, 40, 41, 43, 44, 45, 54, 63, 72, 75, 76, 77, 81, 85, 88, 89, 100, 101, 107, 122, 125, 126, 143, 157 by Madeleine Ridge

Those on pages 1, 15 (lower), 20 (top), 25 (top), 29 (right), 30, 44 (top), 46, 82 (bottom right), 87, 109 (right), 111, 113 (bottom), 117 (top right and middle left), 170 by Horsepix

Those on pages 37, 112, 113 (top) 117 (top line left and centre, middle line right and bottom), 118, 119 by Sue Devereux

All line drawings by Carole Vincer

Points of the pony

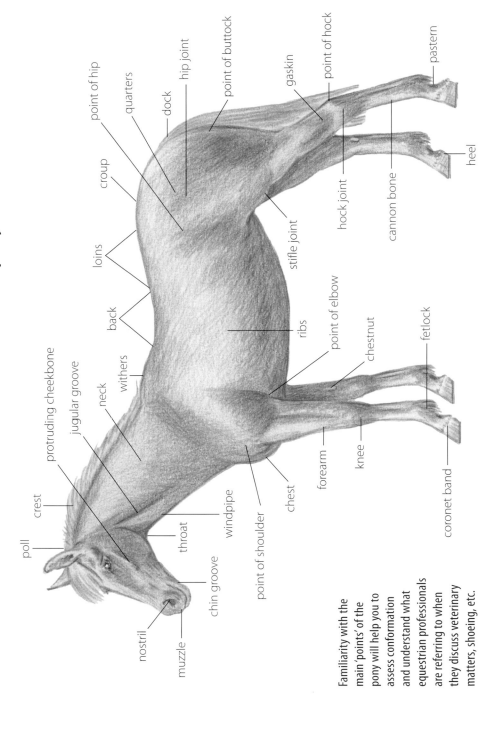

poll
crest
protruding cheekbone
jugular groove
neck
withers
back
loins
croup
point of hip
quarters
dock
hip joint
point of buttock
gaskin
point of hock
pastern
heel
cannon bone
hock joint
stifle joint
ribs
point of elbow
chestnut
fetlock
coronet band
knee
forearm
chest
point of shoulder
windpipe
throat
chin groove
muzzle
nostril

Familiarity with the main 'points' of the pony will help you to assess conformation and understand what equestrian professionals are referring to when they discuss veterinary matters, shoeing, etc.

Introduction

For a child, having their own pony is impossibly exciting. For a parent, however, it can be both a challenge and a huge responsibility. Even the smallest pony can quickly become unmanageable unless he is handled and cared for correctly.

Our comprehensive and practical guide assumes no prior knowledge of the subject and aims to provide you with straightforward information and advice. Once you have mastered the basics you will have the foundation to develop your knowledge and increased confidence in handling and caring for your pony.

Remember that a pony is as much an individual as your child and choosing the right one is the cornerstone to success. Our book guides you through the pitfalls of buying or loaning a pony and finding a home which suits both the pony and your budget and lifestyle. For your child to be able to develop a successful partnership with their pony it is vital you understand his behaviour. By doing this you will be able to accurately anticipate his response to situations and thus learn how to handle him accordingly. As your knowledge increases so will your confidence, which will enable you to control situations and ensure that your child and their pony are able to thrive in a safe environment.

We dispel the myth that dealing with equines is unnecessarily complicated and believe that the key to understanding and managing your pony is a combination of basic knowledge, common sense and confidence.

Above all, our book aims to encourage every parent to get involved and have fun with their child and their pony.

1

A Pony of Your Own

Before deciding whether to commit to buying a pony your child should have been having regular lessons and have reached a reasonable level of competence. You should also be fully aware of the implications, the expense involved and the time required to care for the pony. We also explain the options available if you do not want to buy a pony.

A pony is as much of an individual as your child and choosing the right one is the cornerstone to success.

1.1 WHAT WILL IT COST?

Before you make the final decision to buy a pony, it is sensible to have a realistic idea of what this is going to cost you both financially and in terms of your time. Your budget and individual circumstances will largely influence where you choose to keep the pony and how you arrange for him to be looked after (see Chapter 4). If you are loaning a pony the running costs will be broadly similar. The items referred to in the chart on page 16 (designed to help you budget) are largely mandatory. However, you may also have to allow for tack, equipment, tuition, membership of an organisation (Pony Club), and engaging the services of various professionals for procedures other than those

Pony Club camp is the perfect opportunity for your child to have fun in a learning environment.

listed (e.g. clipping, osteopath and chiropractor, paddock maintenance and transport). We advise that you insure the pony with a minimum of third party cover and have personal accident insurance for your child.

It is important to have a realistic idea of exactly what owning a pony is going to cost financially.

1.2 PRACTICAL CONSIDERATIONS

Having worked out the financial aspects of buying and owning a pony you will need to be clear on how much time you will have available. If the pony is going to be kept on a livery yard, but you are responsible for all of his care, you will need to allocate a minimum of 2 hours a day (this does not include travel to and from the yard and time for riding); this is what will be needed for the essential everyday tasks involved in looking after the pony (see Chapter 7). You will need to visit him in the morning and the afternoon to ensure his safety and well-being. Less

Outgoings	Weekly costs	Monthly costs	Yearly costs
Livery			
Field rent			
Paddock maintenance			
Vaccinations			
Worming			
Farrier			
Dentistry			
Bedding			
Hay/forage			
Hard feed			
Insurance			
TOTAL			

time will be involved if the pony is going to be kept at your home, you are sharing the pony with his owner, or if he is going to be on full livery at a yard and the only time you have to set aside is for your child to ride.

1.3 BUYING

The initial outlay of buying a pony can be expensive. Ponies who are suitable for a child often come at a high premium. It is important that you set a budget at the outset and are not tempted to view ponies who are out of your price range. While there may be some negotiation on price it is unlikely that there will be a significant reduction. Aside from the headline cost you will have to allow for other expenses such as tack and rugs (if not included in the sale price), insurance cover and vetting.

It may be possible to secure the pony on a short-term trial basis, which will allow you the opportunity to further assess his compatibility with your child. If you are having the pony on a trial ensure that you have a written agreement detailing responsibilities of both sides. The seller may require that you insure the pony for the time he is in your care.

Ponies suitable for a young child often come at a high premium.

1.4 LOANING OR SHARING?

Buying is not the only route to having a pony. There are a surprising number of options available which provide the hands-on involvement that your child wants and entail varying levels of financial and time commitments. Alternatives fall broadly into two categories, namely loaning or sharing. A well-structured loan or share arrangement can be the perfect introduction to 'owning' a pony and may provide additional benefits and support that might not otherwise be available if you bought a pony. Also bear in mind that many of the most desirable 'first ponies' rarely appear on the open market: they are either sold by word of mouth or put on loan. The time frame for a young child's first pony is relatively short, as children grow quickly, and therefore you might consider loaning to be a more appropriate option than buying.

Loaning a pony can be a sensible option, especially for first-timers.

Loaning

When loaning a pony it is generally accepted that you will take on both his running costs and his management. If you decide to loan a pony you can go about your search in the same way you would for buying a pony (see Chapter 2). Many charitable organisations including the Blue Cross organise loan programmes for ponies in their care. The loaning process is extremely thorough and includes ridden assessments, a home inspection and periodic check-up visits throughout the term of your loan. As the loan party you will be required to pay a fixed fee (which covers the charity's costs) and once the pony is in your care, assume all responsibility for his costs. You will also be required to sign a loan agreement and have minimum third party insurance.

Another avenue to explore is your local riding centre, which may offer an individual loaning programme. Broadly speaking this offers you the chance to have some involvement with one particular pony.

The expectation is that you pay a certain amount per month and for that you will have an agreed amount of time to ride the pony, perhaps alongside additional benefits such as a number of lessons or hacks. Another option is to loan from a private individual.

Loan agreement

Once you have found a pony the next step is to formalise a loan agreement. This is effectively a contract and should be treated as such. The following are the main areas which should be addressed, although there may be additional aspects detailed which are specific to your particular loan.

- The length of time for which you can loan the pony; whether there is an initial trial period and information regarding terms of notice when returning the pony.

- Details of equipment being included. Generally this will be tack and rugs. Do check the condition of the equipment and draw attention to any existing damage or wear and tear. It is advisable to have an inventory.

- Some ponies are on loan because of their age or an existing medical condition that may limit their involvement in certain activities. This should be clearly outlined in the agreement.

- The financial obligations of both parties should be clearly stated. Generally speaking the borrower assumes responsibility for all costs. However it is best to clarify any potentially contentious issues.

- Details specifying how and where the pony is to be kept.

Pony share

If you are going to share a pony, agreements can be complex and it is important that each party is clear about what is expected in terms of time and financial commitment. A share arrangement generally

Understanding and managing your pony is a combination of basic knowledge, common sense and confidence.

Left: Having fun and growing in confidence is what owning a pony is all about.

involves an agreed amount of access to the pony in exchange for a contribution towards the financial costs and his practical day-to-day care. The pony will almost certainly remain in his current home. Generally speaking you will not have the same freedom you would if you took on a loan pony, but the costs and the involvement required will be less.

2

Choosing a Pony

Ultimately the type of pony you choose for your child will depend on their capability, the job you require the pony to do and the lifestyle you intend for him. However, the most important factor must be that the pony is safe to handle and ride. We explain where to look for a pony, deciphering an advert, making the selection and planning a constructive viewing strategy.

2.1 WHERE TO LOOK

The most logical way to begin your search for a pony is to enquire locally and gradually widen the net if necessary. The advantage of buying a pony on your doorstep is that it may be easier to verify his history and you might have an opportunity to see the pony in action with his current rider. A sensible approach is to contact your child's riding instructor and your local branch of the Pony Club. Also, enquire at your local training centre/riding school, which might come up with a potential match. However, bear in mind that a pony from a riding school may behave differently when taken out of his familiar environment.

The local press, farm and tack shops and relevant commercial advertising sites are also useful places to look. In our opinion you are more likely to find a suitable first or second pony through a private seller. However, should you decide to buy a pony from a reputable dealer you may have a stronger legal position should the pony turn out to be unsuitable. We do not advise that a novice owner buys from either a sale ring or a horse fair. Remember that you may well have to kiss a number of frogs before you find a prince.

2.2 DECIPHERING AN ADVERT

Typically adverts are short – 25/30 words maximum, so understanding exactly what is meant by certain phrases is essential. The pony's height, age, sex and experience level are the crucial criteria, but other terms used may need some explanation. Photographs and video clips are useful but bear in mind that they may not be current or wholly representative of the pony's ability.

Example advert
14.2hh gelding, home-bred, recently backed, rising 4, native, would do well at PC, SJ, ODE, good to BCST, snaffle mouth, bomb-proof, easy to do, first pony.

Translation
14.2hh – this refers to the height of the pony. Horses and ponies (except Shetlands) are measured in hands (one hand = 10.16cm/4in). The measurement is taken from the highest point of the withers in a straight line down to the ground.

Gelding – a castrated male horse/pony.

Home-bred – bred by current owners. Some home-breds may have been over-handled and indulged, which can lead to poor manners, and/or may have only been ridden by one person.

Recently backed – newly broken to saddle and thus extremely inexperienced and not suitable as a first or even a second pony.

Rising 4 – the pony has not yet reached his fourth year and is definitely not suitable for a novice rider.

Native – refers to breeds that are indigenous to the British Isles.

PC, SJ, ODE – these abbreviations stand for Pony Club, Show Jumping, One Day Event.

Good to BCST – good to box (travel), clip, shoe and in traffic.

Snaffle-mouth – a snaffle is the mildest form of bit and indicates that the pony is quiet to ride and easy to stop.

Bomb-proof – a pony who is quiet in all respects and situations. Note: *any* pony is capable of behaving out of character in certain circumstances.

Easy to do – well-mannered and easy to look after.

First pony – implies that he is suitable for a novice rider and is familiar with being handled by a child (so this wouldn't tally with 'recently backed' and 'rising 4', above).

The term 'first pony' should imply that he is suitable to be handled by a child.

2.3 PONY SELECTION

The most important consideration when selecting a pony is that he must be, as far as you can reasonably ascertain, safe to handle, to ride and in traffic. Temperament and experience are particularly relevant criteria when choosing a first pony.

Temperament

The pony should have an equable temperament that will make him suitable for being handled and ridden by a child. He must have good manners, show no signs of aggression and be happy in the company of other ponies.

A pony who is content in his surroundings will be easier to handle and ride.

Experience

As a general rule of thumb a novice partnership – pony and rider – is a recipe for disaster. The more experienced the pony, the more likely he is to be suitable for a young or inexperienced child. For example if the pony has been successfully ridden by children of a similar age and ability to your own he may well prove to be ideal.

An ideal child's pony should be calm, well-mannered and easy to handle.

Size

Never buy a pony with the intention of your child growing into him. A child will find it hard to progress and may become anxious and nervous if the pony is too big for them to ride and to handle comfortably and safely.

Type

Your personal preference and your budget will probably dictate whether you choose a pure-bred or a pony with mixed breeding. Primarily you are looking for a pony who is physically robust and has a reliable temperament. In our opinion, temperament and conformation are more important than the pony's breeding.

Age

The age of the pony will have a direct impact on his suitability for the job and, ultimately, on your exit strategy. Older ponies are ideal for children but if the pony is 20-plus he may suffer from an ongoing condition such as arthritis or a respiratory complaint, which may require therapeutic maintenance doses of drugs. A very young pony will almost certainly lack the level of experience compatible with a novice rider. The pony's passport will have a record of his foaling date.

Asking the right questions

The more you know about the pony the more reliable your judgement will be when making a final decision. Owners will rarely lie but they may not necessarily volunteer information about certain aspects of the pony. Therefore, it is a good idea to ask the following questions.

Reasons for sale? These can be many and varied, therefore you need to be happy with the explanation. The most straightforward reason is that the child has outgrown the pony.

How long has the pony been in his current home? If he has been passed down the family and is now outgrown, or has been with his present owners for at least a year, this is definitely a plus point. If a pony has only been in his current home a few months you need to find out why he is being moved on so swiftly. Bear in mind that you may not necessarily be told the whole truth and will therefore need to read between the lines.

What has the pony been doing? Does his recent ridden history match what you imagine your child might be able to do with him? It is also worth asking how experienced the current rider was when they first had the pony.

Is he good in traffic? Find out whether the pony is regularly ridden on the roads and what sort of traffic he encounters. A pony who is unreliable in traffic is a danger not only to your child but also to other road users.

It is imperative that you find a pony who is safe to ride out on the roads.

Will he hack alone? This is more relevant when buying a pony for an older, more experienced child.

Is he easy to handle, catch and shoe? A pony suitable for a child must have good manners, which will make him safe to handle and easy to deal with. However, if the pony becomes upset in specific situations, such as when being shod or clipped, these are points that definitely should be considered but may not rule the pony out if he is good in all other respects.

Ask questions such as 'Is the pony easy to catch?'

Is he easy to load and will he travel in a trailer and a lorry in company, or alone? If you have your own transport and are intending to go out and about then it is important that you are able to load the pony safely. Knowing what type of transport the pony is happiest travelling in and whether he will travel alone are questions you will need to ask so that you can make a decision on the pony's suitability.

How is the pony currently kept? This will have a direct bearing on where you are planning to keep him. For example, if he prefers to live

It is worth finding out whether the pony is used to travelling in a trailer or a lorry.

Some ponies prefer to live out year round, and most will prefer companionship.

out and you plan to stable him at a livery yard with minimal turnout he may not settle in his new environment.

Is he up to date with vaccinations, worming and dental checks? All vaccinations should be recorded in his passport and signed by a vet.

Does the pony have any 'vices'? What were traditionally called 'vices' and are now usually termed 'stereotypical behaviours' are recognised patterns of repeated negative behaviour and include box-walking, crib-biting, wind-sucking and weaving. It is important to remember that while these cannot be cured they can generally be managed, usually by minimising the situations that the pony finds stressful and having a routine for him that involves a large amount of turnout.

Does the pony show any aggressive behaviour? A pony who has a history of biting or kicking his handler is definitely unsuitable.

Is there an existing or recurring medical condition which may affect the pony's management? If he suffers from laminitis, Cushing's disease, sweet itch, or is prone to colic (see Chapter 12) you will need to take these into account and discuss them with your vet before you go ahead with the purchase.

What is included in the sale price? Be clear about what equipment, if any, is being offered in the sale price.

A pony might look attractive, but temperament and conformation are so much more important.

2.4 VIEWING THE PONY

We would advise that you seek a professional opinion before buying the pony, preferably from someone who knows you and your child's skill levels – probably your child's riding instructor. You will need to negotiate an appropriate fee. However, while we would always advise seeking such professional advice, it is worth remembering that the advantage you have over an expert is an understanding of your child and what you expect of the pony and how he will fit in with your family life. Knowing exactly what you want to ask, how to interpret the answers and what you want to see your child do when you view the pony, will arm you with the confidence to help you make the right choice. The following points will help you structure your first visit and give you a rough time scale which will keep the viewing focused and prevent you wasting time. An hour should be sufficient for you to assess the pony. Most owners will be happy for you to make a second visit.

- Ask if it is possible to have the pony ridden by his current rider before your child gets on board; this approach allows you to gauge the suitability of the pony.

- Arrange for the use of a school, or a small paddock, so that the pony can be ridden in a controlled environment.

- If your child is happy whilst riding the pony in an enclosed space you will then need to take the pony out on a short hack, which will give you the opportunity to see how he behaves in traffic.

Watch the pony being ridden by his current rider before your child gets on.

Below: Riding out in company will help the pony to settle.

- If you want to see the pony jump then you need to say so in advance so that the owners can arrange for jump equipment to be available.

First impressions

An ideal child's pony should be calm, relaxed and well-mannered to handle. This is best demonstrated by watching how he behaves when being caught, in either the stable or the paddock, groomed and tacked up. Your child may be able to get involved at this point – however, since everything in this scenario is unfamiliar, the combination of an excitable child and an unknown pony may not be ideal. It is also worth comparing the description in the advert to the pony in front of you. During your visit find out whether he is predominantly grass-kept or stabled and if he is kept alone or in company, as this will directly impact on whether he will fit happily into the lifestyle you intend for him. If you haven't already done so, ask about the pony's recent history, the reasons for sale and whether the pony has any relevant medical issues.

It is useful to see a pony being tacked up when viewing.

Riding the pony

At the risk of stating the obvious, your child's ability to ride the pony is the crucial part of the exercise. Their level of competence and circumstances on the day will ultimately govern how much ridden work they are able to do. An apprehensive child or adverse weather conditions should be taken into account when planning your viewing strategy. Even if your child appears confident, you should always err on the side of caution. Remember that they are riding a new pony in unfamiliar surroundings and possibly (though ideally not) without an instructor for the first time. With this in mind you must satisfy yourself that your child is compatible with the pony. Understandably some children may be nervous or reluctant to ride in an unfamiliar situation and if this is the case you could arrange for your child to have a lesson. You may be able to take your child's instructor with you, or you could ask the owners if they could recommend a suitable teacher. Having a lesson will help your child put the pony through his paces in the safest possible setting. This is in an ideal situation; however, if your life is not ideal, here are some useful points to consider.

- Remember that it can be quite scary riding an unfamiliar pony in front of other people so give your child a chance to settle. Allowing your child time to relax and get used to the pony will give you the opportunity to assess whether you think they are a reasonably good match.

- The pony must be ridden on both reins (this means both directions) in walk and trot. If the child feels happy to do so, they should also canter the pony.

- The pony's jumping ability may well be important and, if it is, you should, at the very least, see the pony jump with his current rider.

- If your child is happy to do so, you should ask if it is possible to take the pony on a short hack. How the pony behaves in traffic is a vital safety consideration. However, if you are not happy with your child riding a strange pony on the road you could ask if the owner will take the pony out while you accompany them on foot. Hacking the pony out will also allow you to see how he behaves in a less controlled environment.

Decision time

We advise that you give yourself 24 hours before making a decision. Ideally arrange with the seller to contact them the following day. This gives you time to verify any information that came to light during the viewing and crucially allows you to come to a conclusion without being pressurised by either the owners or your child. You will also have time to organise a vetting, insurance and transport (see Chapter 3), if you do not have your own.

Essentially you are looking for a pony who has a reliable temperament and who is physically robust.

Keep safe

- It is worth bringing a pair of stirrup irons (safety irons) and leathers (see Chapter 14) which fit your child. Have them properly fitted to your child's foot while they are wearing their riding boots. This will avoid a situation where your child is trying a strange pony in irons that are not the right size and leathers which could be unsafe.

The tack used must fit your child: here, a correctly fitting stirrup iron with appropriate length stirrup leather.

- Your child must wear a riding hat, riding boots and a body protector (see Chapter 15).

- If going out on a hack, ensure your child is wearing a reflective tabard.

- Consider putting the pony on a lead rein when hacking out even if it is just for the first 5 or 10 minutes.

3

Practicalities

When you have decided on the pony you want to buy there are a number of practical issues that will need to be dealt with immediately. Having the pony looked at by a vet, a process known as vetting, is advisable. You will also need to organise some form of insurance cover and transport. There are also the practical aspects of settling your pony into his new home.

3.1 VETTING

This is a process by which the pony you have selected is examined by a vet, who will tell you whether there are any ongoing medical conditions or old injuries that could inhibit the pony's ability to do the job you want him to do.

It is worth noting that this report is a professional opinion, not a guarantee of soundness. When booking a vetting you need to be aware that they come in grades or stages numbered 1 to 5, 5 being the most thorough and costly. The most basic vetting will assess the pony's wind, heart and eyes.

Why have a vetting?

Vetting is a procedure that buys you peace of mind. However, it does come at a price. You may decide that paying potentially up to 10 per cent of his purchase price only for you not to buy the pony eventually is a price worth paying. However, you may feel that if you are buying a 12hh pony for £1,000 it may only be worthwhile paying for a basic vetting, or possibly not having one at all. Alternatively, if you are paying a lot of money for the pony we would advise you to have a thorough vetting. A basic vetting will assess the general health of the pony as well as his heart, lungs and eyesight. These key points cannot be seen by the layperson and therefore this would be a wise choice to consider.

A vet will examine the pony's heart with a stethoscope.

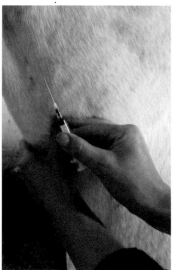

A full vetting may include taking a blood sample.

Costs and who pays for it

As mentioned, the price of vetting will depend on which stage you are having, 1 (very basic) being the cheapest and 5 (very thorough) the most expensive. It will also depend on which veterinary practice you use and how far you are asking them to travel. All practices will have a list of stages and prices.

As you will be paying for the vetting, and you still have to pay even if the pony 'fails' the vet, you need to be as sure as possible that you have, in all other respects, selected the right pony for you before you proceed. For your own peace of mind we advise that, if you are planning on having the pony vetted, you go ahead with this even if you are told that the pony has recently undergone a vetting.

Selecting a vet

You can choose any veterinary practice you like to undertake a vetting, so long as it has an equine division. If you are expecting the vet to travel considerable distances to carry out the vetting you may be charged travelling expenses.

In order to avoid any conflict of interest, it is advisable not to use the pony's current vet for this procedure.

Vetting procedure

In order to assess the pony's suitability the vet will need to know the purpose of the purchase; he will then examine the pony with this in mind and give an opinion on the pony's suitability. At the end of the examination the vet will highlight any aspects of the animal's health that he considers relevant and give his professional opinion as to whether the pony is suitable. Ultimately, however, it is your decision whether you choose to heed the advice you are given.

When you have booked your vetting you need to let the owners know if you require any specific facilities in order for the vet to carry out the examination. This is particularly relevant if the pony lives in a muddy field in the middle of nowhere.

We advise that you attend the assessment so that the vet can go through the report and explain their findings. This will give you the opportunity to clarify any points you are uncertain about.

3.2 INSURANCE

Whether you decide to insure the pony for veterinary fees and death is a personal choice; however, we strongly advise that, at the very least, you have third party public liability insurance. In most cases this cover will be requisite if you are going to keep the pony on a commercial livery yard. It is generally included as a basic in most insurance policies. However, if your child is a member of the Pony Club or the BHS you will automatically receive this cover as part of your membership. Specialist equine insurers, or divisions within general insurance companies, will be able to provide you with a full range of policies. Depending on the price you are paying for the pony you may also be required to provide a veterinary report.

3.3 PASSPORT

Since 2003 all equines have been required by law to have a valid equine passport and you must ensure that the current owners give you the pony's passport when you have completed the purchase.

It is a legal requirement for all horses and ponies to have a valid equine passport.

3.4 NEW PONY, NEW HOME

Unless you have your own transport, and are competent at towing (Chapter 16), we advise that you use a professional transporter to move the pony to his new home. It is always preferable to arrange for the pony to arrive during the day so that you have time to settle him in. To make the pony's move as seamless as possible there are a number of key areas which should be considered.

Diet

If the pony is on good-quality hay/or haylage, try to buy some of the seller's current supply so that you can feed it alongside your own. Follow a similar policy with any hard feed (see Chapter 8), allowing you to gradually change one element of the pony's diet at a time.

Social interaction

Introducing the pony to his new field companions needs to be approached carefully. Turn him out in a small paddock adjacent to his future field mates to allow them to interact whilst minimising the risk of injury. If this is not possible, turn him out with a quiet companion to allow him to adjust to his surroundings.

Turning your pony out with a quiet companion will help him settle in his new environment.

Management routine

If your pony is used to being turned out in the day and kept in at night it is worth mimicking this until he has settled. This allows you then to make further changes with minimal disruption. It is important to remember that it is the predictability of his routine that will prevent him from becoming stressed. Ponies are creatures of habit.

Worming programme

We would advise you to ask the previous owners about the pony's worming regime; when he was last wormed and with what product. That said, it is always prudent to worm a pony on his arrival at his new home. You will then be able to compile a comprehensive worming programme adhering to manufacturer's guidelines. It is worth noting that most yards have a worming policy with which you will be expected to comply.

Worming your pony regularly will ensure you reduce his worm burden.

4

Home Sweet Home

Selecting a suitable home to keep your pony will be largely dictated by location, budget and the time you have available to look after him, and suitable facilities. In this chapter we discuss how to choose between the different options available to you and list the priorities in the basic order of importance. As it is unlikely that any one solution will be perfect, it is sensible to list and prioritise your requirements to ensure that any compromises you make are sensibly managed and do not prejudice safety.

4.1 GRAZING

Suitable grazing is the linchpin in any decision of where to keep a pony. Listed below are the criteria to use when assessing potential turnout. The management of a grass-kept pony is explained in Chapter 7.

Fencing. The paddock must have safe and robust fencing either in the form of a well-built stone wall, minimum height of 110cm (3ft 6in), secure post and rail fencing or a thick, mature, rail-reinforced hedge. The latter must not include yew, privet, laurel, oak or laburnum, which are poisonous to ponies. If a poisonous tree is an integral part of the hedge line it should be fenced off in such a way as not to allow the ponies to reach it. The access gate needs to be secure and to open inwards.

Top left: A post and rail fence line will require regular maintenance.

Top right: A well-maintained five-bar gate.

Left: A sprung gate hitch.

Above: Mature hedgerow provides shelter and an effective fencing option.

Dimensions. If your pony is going to be turned out all year you will need just under a hectare (approximately 2 acres) for one pony and approximately 0.5 hectare (a further acre) for every additional pony. If he is going to be stabled with access to turnout, 0.5 hectare (1 acre) per pony is adequate.

It is important to note that ponies are herd animals and are generally happier if kept in a small group, or within sight of other ponies. In the case of group turnout it is preferable for them to be separated into groups of mares and geldings. This helps to prevent bullying and squabbling amongst field companions.

Ponies are herd animals and are happier when kept in small groups.

Access to water. There should be a constant supply of clean, fresh water (not a stagnant pond or a stream). Ideally a well-maintained, self-filling trough situated on hard standing away from both the gate and overhanging trees.

Automatic water troughs provide a constant supply of fresh water but will need to be checked daily.

Shelter. Some form of shelter that offers protection from the prevailing wind is essential. This can be natural or artificial – a sturdy hedge or a man-made windbreak. A roofed field shelter offers extra protection from severe weather, but it must be three-sided to minimise the possibility of a pony being cornered by his field companions.

Management of grazing. The field must be free from plants deemed to be poisonous to ponies. The most common of these are ragwort,

A man-made shelter should be positioned out of the prevailing wind.

foxglove, deadly nightshade, hemlock, bracken, yew, laburnum, laurel and oak.

The regular removal of droppings is essential to keep a pony's 'worm burden' to a minimum as all equines harbour some quantity of parasitic worm (see Chapter 9). This will also prevent the development of 'roughs' (patches of thick, unpalatable grass and weeds) and 'lawns' (the closely grazed parts of the field). To avoid areas becoming damaged (commonly termed 'poached') a programme of resting/rotating/re-seeding the grazing is advisable.

Below left: Fields should be free from poisonous plants such as foxgloves.

Below centre: Laburnum is another poisonous plant: seen here in flower, it will have long, thin seed pods in the autumn.

Below right: Ragwort is highly toxic and must be removed at the roots.

A stable door should have bolts top and bottom, and a roof overhang will prevent water dripping directly into the stable.

4.2 STABLING

Ideally the stable should have the following minimum dimensions: size 3 x 3.6m (10 x 12ft); height 3.6m (12ft), preferably with a pitched roof; door width 1.37m (4ft 6in); height of lower door between 1.2–1.5m (4–5ft). There are lower doors available on the market that would be more suitable for a smaller pony. It should be well ventilated, but not draughty, have a good overhang of roof and adequate drainage. Windows should be protected on the inside with a metal grid, and doors should open outwards. Lighting and associated cabling within a stable must be enclosed to prevent any possibility of a pony seizing it with his teeth or otherwise damaging it and endangering himself. Light fittings with toughened glass that are designed for outdoor use are advisable.

Stables should be in a good state of repair; for example doors can often drop on their hinges, causing them to be difficult to secure as the bolts and catches no longer line up. The box should have one tie-up ring on a side wall to secure the pony and a second one on the front wall (at

This yard has been designed so that the horses can see one another.

a minimum height of 1.5m (5ft) to secure a haynet. The general layout of the yard should be such that you and your child can handle the pony safely. The management of a stable-kept pony is detailed in Chapter 7.

4.3 FACILITIES AND SERVICES

For many first-time owners access to credible help and professional advice will be crucial. This, coupled with the provision of suitable facilities and equipment, may determine your ultimate choice of a home.

For novice owners, being on a well-run livery yard with access to professional help can be advantageous.

Types of livery

Generally speaking livery is broken down into three categories: full, part and DIY. The last refers to the rental of facilities on offer, with all aspects of the pony's care and welfare being the responsibility of you as the owner. Part livery commonly includes the provision of some services such as mucking out/turning out/bringing in/feeding (although the last may involve simply putting in feeds made up by the owner). The most comprehensive package will be in the form of full livery, in which all aspects of your pony's day-to-day care will be carried out by the yard's staff, although schooling and exercising the pony are likely to be charged separately. It is worth noting that professional costs such as farriery, dentistry and veterinary will not be included in any livery package.

Many livery yards operate a combined management system where ponies are stabled but have daily turnout.

Assessing facilities

Whatever form of livery you decide upon, the following facilities can be considered desirable.

- Access to a weatherproof, rodent-free barn or other suitable building allowing the storage of bedding and hay/haylage.

- A well-ventilated feed room of an adequate size to allow feed to be stored in individual bins, which helps keep it fresh and prevents contamination with other products and rodent infestation.

- The provision of a secure, lockable tack room.

- A dry, covered area for the storing and drying of rugs.

- An all-weather exercise area – either an indoor or an outdoor arena (with floodlights).

- Safe access and adequate parking for vehicles and the availability of secure standing for trailers and lorries.

- Off-road hacking.

- Professional services – for example, tuition, transport, clipping and schooling.

Above: An all-weather arena with lights means your child will be able to ride after school during the winter months.

Left: A horse-walker is a useful facility to have on a yard because it means your pony can be exercised in circumstances when it may not be practical to ride him – for example, if the fields and roads are icy.

4.4 CONTRACTS, INSURANCE AND YARD POLICIES

A well-written contract is a hallmark of a professionally run yard. Areas to which you need to pay close attention are payment, notice period and insurance requirements.

Some insurance policies can be quite specific with regard to security measures relating to both the pony and your equipment.

In addition you should also be aware of the yard's vaccination policy, worming regime, opening hours, any restrictions on visiting instructors and whether there are extra charges for such things as winter lighting in the arena, parking a trailer and hiring the arena for sole use.

Keep safe

- You may wish to consider having your pony micro-chipped, which will allow him to be reliably identified with the use of a micro-chip reader. The micro-chip number will be recorded on his passport. This procedure is carried out by a vet.

- Even if your insurance policy does not stipulate it, a prudent measure is to label your tack/equipment with your postcode. One way of doing this is to have it stamped into the leather on the underside of the saddle flap and cheekpiece. Alternatively you could contact your local police authority and ask for the most effective way of security-tagging your equipment.

- For added security use a chain and padlock on both the hinge and latch end of the paddock gate – although you will have to ask permission from the land owner or livery yard manager.

- Trailer/lorries are vulnerable to opportunistic theft. With this in mind use a trailer hitch lock or wheel clamp on your trailer/lorry.

5

Handling

The foundation of a successful partnership with the pony lies in consistent and correct handling. Your child may love him to bits and be all set to join the local branch of the Pony Club, but if you are unable to handle the pony safely and competently all this will count for little. A few well-placed instructions and a sound understanding of the most effective way to handle your pony will enable you to maintain control and ensure a safe environment. For a child the enjoyment they experience when being with their pony is hard to match. For a parent, conversely, these are potentially stressful and anxious occasions. In this chapter we outline the fundamental techniques required in three key areas: handling the pony in the paddock, in his stable and when he is being ridden.

5.1 IN THE PADDOCK

Ideally you should wear gloves whenever you are leading a pony. This will prevent you getting rope burn if he pulls away suddenly, and also improves your grip on the rope. Also, when getting to know your new pony, wearing a hard hat is recommended.

Catching and turning out a pony in a paddock can present you with a number of issues. It may be that you have a pony who is very keen to get to the field, or one who doesn't want to come in. You might have to walk some distance (possibly down a public highway) to the field, negotiate a tricky gate or have field companions to deal with.

Putting on a headcollar

A headcollar fastens with a buckle on the left-hand side and has a hoop or ring under the pony's chin to attach the lead rope. Approach your pony on his left side, towards his shoulder, and place the rope over his neck. Hold the noseband open with both hands and slip it over his nose, then bring the long strap over his head behind his ears with your right hand. Finally, fasten the buckle with the end of the strap tucked in so that it cannot come undone.

It is best practice to approach the pony from the left-hand side whenever circumstances allow this.

Top left: Offer the noseband of the headcollar to the pony.

Top right: Move the noseband over his nose, taking care to stay on his left.

Above: Pass the long strap of the headcollar over the pony's head with your right hand, keeping the buckle in your left hand.

Right: Fasten the buckle on his left side.

Taking the lead

Hold the lead rope just below the clip with your right hand and hold the other end in the left hand. Never wrap the rope round your hand: if the

pony tries to run away you will get dragged and are likely to be seriously injured. Lead the pony from his left side, staying level with his shoulder and allowing him to walk freely. Staying in this position will enable you to have more control and lessen the likelihood of the pony spinning and accelerating away from you. If you allow the pony to get too far ahead of you, you will end up level with his hip/hindquarters. This position affords you very little control and puts you at the risk of being kicked. If you walk too far in front, the pony could stop or run backwards or, if he is spooked, he could run straight into you. Always turn the pony *away* from you as he is then less likely to tread on your feet.

Above: Always wear gloves when leading to prevent rope burn if the pony pulls away.

Right: Never stand at the pony's stifle (hind leg) area as you are more likely to be kicked.

Above: Keep the yard tidy to prevent equipment being hazardous when leading your pony.

Right: A Chifney can be used to lead a pony who is quite strong to handle.

Dealing with gates

Halt the pony when you reach the gate. Once you have opened the gate, apply steady pressure to the pony's left shoulder so he moves away from you. Try to keep hold of the gate with one hand so that it does not shut on you or swing too far back. Stay close to the pony's shoulder and allow him space so that he can turn and move around you. See the photo sequence overleaf.

Top left: Keep control of the gate with one hand.

Top right: Ensure the gate is open wide enough for the pony to pass through safely.

Lower left: Always turn the pony away from you.

Lower right: When closing the gate, keep the pony away from the gate hitch so that he cannot get caught up in it.

Turning out

Once you are in the paddock, secure the gate and turn the pony so that he is facing the fence line. Avoid doing this where you can get cornered. A useful tip when removing the headcollar is to give the pony a treat, which will encourage him to drop his head and stand still until you have removed the headcollar and moved safely out of his way.

Field companions

When a pony is used to being turned out in company it can be difficult to get him from the paddock by himself. You may be able to arrange with the other owners to bring in all the ponies at the same time. Alternatively you could construct a large pen around the gate area using electric tape and plastic stakes. This will help you to separate your pony safely from the group before you open the gate.

Common problems

If your pony is difficult to catch there are a number of ways you can solve this.

- Establish a routine, as ponies are generally easier to catch if there is a 'usual' time when they come in.

- When you go into the field, keep the headcollar out of sight and look at the ground as you approach him. This should allow you to get close enough so that you can put the rope round his neck and then put on the headcollar.

- Try bringing him in from the field and giving him a small feed. This will mean he won't associate being caught with just being worked.

- If he is out in company you can ask the owners of other ponies if you can bring the other ponies in first. This approach normally works as most ponies do not like being left out on their own. To make this work safely you will need someone to help you.

Some ponies are happy to be caught but will then refuse to move. This behaviour is known as 'planting'. If this happens, try the following.

- Stay close to the pony's left shoulder and push him sideways, which will unbalance him so he has to take a step. You must be quick to keep him moving otherwise he may take root again. Do not stand in front of him and pull as this may make him walk backwards or rear (stand up).

- Use the slack of the lead rope to flick the pony's side, which should encourage him to move forward. For this to be effective you need to stay close to his left shoulder and apply pressure with your elbow.

- You may need to have another person with you who can stand at a safe distance behind the pony and clap their hands or wave their arms. Ponies will generally move away from any noise.

Keep safe

- Resist the temptation to physically push a reluctant pony from behind as this puts you in an extremely dangerous position.

- Never take a bucket of feed into a paddock to catch the pony. With more than one animal in the field, a feeding frenzy may develop which could result in you or your pony getting kicked.

A pressure halter.

- If you find the pony too strong to lead you can use a bridle (without the martingale or breastplate attachment). Alternatively, there are specialist headcollars that provide extra control by applying pressure primarily over the top of the pony's head or on the chin area. (Use these for leading only, not for tying up.)

5.2 IN THE STABLE

A pony's natural instinct is one of flight or fight, therefore handling him in a confined space such as a stable requires a measured and thoughtful approach. Your child may well be more confident around the pony than you are, but they may not be as aware of how the pony is interacting with them. By using your voice to reassure the pony and keeping your movements smooth and unhurried you will help him to feel safe and relaxed in his environment.

Always talk to your pony as you approach him in his stable.

Traditional nylon headcollar with adjustable noseband.

Tying up and handling

Always talk to your pony when you enter his box and remember to shut the door behind you. Approach him from the side so that he can see you clearly. Keep talking to him and, if he turns away, do not be tempted to chase him round the stable. Stand by the pony's left shoulder and stroke him gently before you put on his headcollar. To move your pony around always push him away from you, which will prevent him standing on your feet or knocking you over. In order to be safe, avoid walking behind the pony or getting caught between him and a wall or the door.

Always attach the lead rope to the headcollar with the clip facing away from the chin.

The safest place to tie a pony is parallel to the door, which means you can approach from the side and are less likely to startle him. Avoid tying him up either facing the door, where he could escape, or at the back of the box where you will have to approach his hindquarters.

Ideally there should be a tie ring with a piece of baler twine attached. Thread the rope through the string and secure with a quick-release knot. If the pony panics and pulls back the string will break and he is less likely to injure himself. The rope should be long enough to allow him to move his head from side to side, but not so long that he can get caught in it.

Securing a lead rope *Top left:* Thread the rope through the baler twine. *Lower left:* Thread the slack through the loop.

Top right: Make a loop with the rope. *Lower right:* Pull tight to secure.

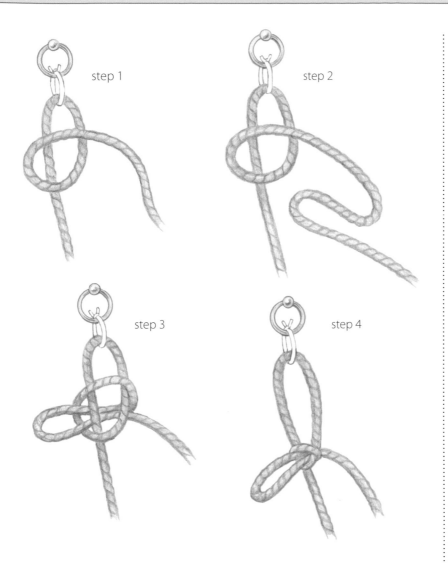

step 1

step 2

step 3

step 4

How to tie a quick-release knot.

Whenever you need to handle the pony in the stable you should always tie him up. This avoids potentially dangerous situations such as the pony getting caught up in the mucking-out tools or escaping out of the door if you have left it open.

Leaving or returning to the stable

Ensure the stable door is wide open before you lead your pony through it. Walk slightly ahead of him, which will keep you in control and also avoid you getting pinned against the door frame. Keeping the pony straight will reduce the risk of him banging his hip as he walks through the narrow space. If the pony is reluctant to go into the stable you can put the light on, which will make it more inviting.

Keep safe

- To prevent a pony barging out of the stable, attach a stable chain, or similar product, which stretches across the doorway.

- Avoid tying the pony up to gates, doors or haynets.

- Wherever you tie up your pony ensure you attach the rope to a piece of string.

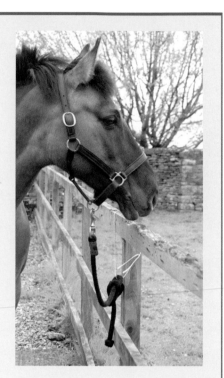

Always tie the pony to a piece of string so that if he pulls back the string will break.

5.3 WHEN THE PONY IS BEING RIDDEN

If your child is still on the lead rein you will need to be confident in handling the pony in a number of different situations and environments. Applying effective techniques will enable you to maintain control of the pony and keep both your child and yourself safe. When leading a pony, put a well-fitting headcollar under the bridle. This gives you control but allows the rider to influence the direction and speed of the pony. You could also use a Newmarket chain, which clips onto both bit rings and has a hoop in the middle onto which you clip a rope. This will enable you to exert pressure on the bit if necessary while still giving your child a degree of influence over the pony.

Left: A well-fitting headcollar under the bridle.

Above: Rope attached to the bit for leading (photographed from below).

Mounting

Start as you mean to go on and avoid lifting the child onto the pony. First check that the girth is tight. If your child mounts from a block, stand on the right-hand side of the pony so that you can stop the pony moving off before the child has got into the saddle. You can also hold the stirrup to prevent the saddle from slipping. Should you need to leg your child onto the pony we advise you clip on a lead rope to maintain control while they mount. See photos of mounting methods overleaf.

Dismounting

We advise that you support or steady the younger or more inexperienced child with your right hand as they dismount. This allows you to control the pony with your left. When leading the pony back to the

Mounting from a block

Top left: Rider mounts from the left-hand side. Puts the left foot in the stirrup, the reins in left hand and places right hand on the far side of the waist of the saddle.

Top right: Rider springs up and clears the back of the pony with the right leg.

Left: Rider sits in saddle and puts right foot in stirrup.

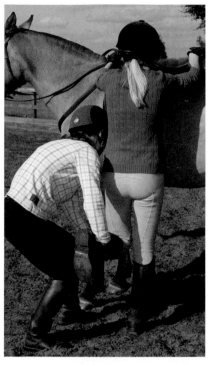

Mounting with a leg-up

Top left: Rider stands on left side of the pony, holds the reins and front of the saddle in their left hand and the right hand holds the seat on the far side. The rider bends their left knee and the assistant has their left hand on the rider's left knee and their right hand on the front of the ankle.

Top right: Rider jumps up on the count of three and the assistant lifts.

Lower left: The rider's right leg clears the back of the saddle.

Lower right: Rider sits down in the saddle and puts feet into the stirrup irons.

stable unclip the lead rope and take the reins over his head, which will prevent them becoming tangled or caught. The exception to this is if he is wearing a running martingale, in which case hold the reins about 15cm (6in) below the bit. Remember to lead the pony from the left side.

School sense

When leading the pony into an arena turn him around the gate as you close it, which will allow you to remain in control of both the pony and the gate. Lead the pony from his inside so that you don't get pinned against the boundary fence. When you change the rein (direction) you will also need to change the side you lead from. If there are other people using the arena pass them left to left and use the inner track if you are walking, or if you wish to halt. Take the pony into the middle of the arena if your child is either mounting or dismounting. This is also the safest place to be if you need to alter your child's stirrup leathers or tighten the girth.

In company

Even quiet ponies can become quite animated when in group situations such as a Pony Club rally or a show. If you need to keep hold of the pony until he settles you should use a lead rope rather than holding the reins, which may destabilise your child and put you in a dangerous position. Take care to remain level with his shoulder and avoid coming into close proximity with other people and ponies. A useful technique to settle the pony is to walk him quietly in a large circle rather than insisting that he remains stationary. Always wear gloves when leading and try to remain calm and unhurried. This will help both the pony and child to relax and enjoy their day.

Leading a pony on the road

When taking your child out on a hack it is advisable to choose your route and time carefully. Even the most reliable pony may become unsettled by

Ponies and riders are relaxed, allowing them to enjoy their day.

When leading the pony you should be between him and the traffic.

excessive traffic. Attach the lead rope to the left-hand bit ring and thread it through the right, thus giving you maximum control. Your child should always ride on the left-hand side of the road but you must lead the pony from his right-hand side so that you are between the pony and the traffic. It is not permitted to ride on the pavement or public footpaths.

Ponies are easily frightened and can take exception to all manner of objects, particularly pigs, llamas and heavy farm machinery. If anything like this happens, turn the pony's head away from whatever has upset him and keep walking. Use your voice to reassure him.

Keep safe

- Always lead a pony in a bridle.

- To ensure that you are seen by other road users it is advisable that you and your child wear a high-visibility tabard.

- Use clear hand signals so that road users know what you are about to do.

Left: Reflectives should be worn when riding on the road.

Above: Choose your route carefully to avoid heavy traffic.

6

Grooming

Grooming a pony is a rewarding and achievable task that even the smallest child can enjoy. They will develop a bond with their pony and gradually learn to become more confident and competent when they are handling him. We outline how to groom the pony safely and explain the techniques of pulling and trimming and how to plait the mane and tail.

Grooming will help your child bond with their pony.

6.1 ESSENTIAL KIT AND ITS USE

The following items may be used in the grooming process.

Body brush – removes grease and dust from the face, clipped areas of the coat and a short summer coat. Use to brush out the mane and the tail. Don't use on a pony who lives out as the soft, close-set bristles will remove the natural grease from his coat.

Dandy brush – the long, stiff bristles are effective at removing dry mud. Do not use on clipped or sensitive areas.

Hoof pick – removes mud and stones out of the hoof.

Mitt – different types are available and are useful for removing dried mud and sweat, particularly around the face and ears.

Scrubbing brush – use for scrubbing hooves and feet.

Metal curry comb – use to clean the body brush.

Rubber curry comb – removes loose hair and is particularly useful when the pony is moulting. Do not use on sensitive areas of his body.

Plastic curry comb – removes dried mud from thick winter coats.

Sponges – ideally three sponges (different colours) one for the eyes and the nose, one for the dock and the third for general bathing.

Below left: The body brush removes grease and dust and can also be used to brush out the pony's mane and tail. Clean the brush with a metal curry comb.

Above right: A rubber curry comb removes loose hair but should not be used on sensitive parts of the pony's body.

Right: Clean the eyes and nostrils with a sponge. Keep a separate one for sponging the dock area.

Hoof oil – use sparingly. Clean and wipe dry the hoof before applying the oil.

Comb – use to pull a mane and tail and to section the mane before plaiting.

Clean grooming brushes regularly in warm water with a small amount of washing-up liquid (taking care to rinse thoroughly). Leave the brushes to dry in a warm place. Avoid the bristles remaining wet for long periods as this can rot the handles of wooden brushes.

6.2 HOW TO GROOM

Regular grooming will ensure your pony has a well-maintained coat and will promote good skin condition. While thorough grooming is most effective when done after the pony has been exercised, you will also need to brush him before he is ridden, to remove mud or dirt, especially where the saddle and bridle fit.

Top: Use a comb to brush out the mane before plaiting or pulling to remove knots and mud.

However, if your pony lives out, while you will need to clean off the mud, you should not brush him excessively as this will remove the natural grease in his coat which helps to keep him warm and dry.

1. Tie up the pony using a quick-release knot.

2. Pick out his feet into a skip bucket. (Chapter 10 describes how to pick up the feet.) Use the hoof pick from heel to toe, taking care to avoid the frog, which is the triangular structure in the centre of the foot. See photos overleaf.

3. Encourage your child to brush the pony using long, even strokes that go with lie of the coat. Groom in a logical fashion, starting with his head and working back.

Lower: Keep your grooming kit clean by regularly washing the brushes in warm water and washing-up liquid.

You will need to pick out your pony's feet at least twice a day.

Whenever you are around the pony ensure your movements are predictable so as not to startle him.

Right: Always stand at the side of the pony rather than directly behind him.

Far right: Holding a hind limb correctly.

4. When brushing the pony's face untie the rope and either leave it threaded through the string or hold it. This will prevent him from pulling back and becoming agitated. You can unbuckle the headcollar and secure it round his neck. Remember to re-tie the rope and put the headcollar back on when you have finished brushing his head.

5. Brush out his mane and tail using either a body brush or a specially designed 'hair brush'. Stand to the side of the pony and hold up the whole tail in one hand, brushing out small amounts at a time.

6. Wipe under his dock and clean his eyes and nose with the relevant sponges (see above).

Washing the pony

It is not ideal to wash the pony regularly from head to toe as this depletes his coat's natural weatherproofing qualities. Instead, target the areas of his coat that are particularly dirty. To wash the pony's tail, place it in a bucket of warm water, using a sponge to wet the top of it. Use a mild shampoo and work the lather into the hairs. It is important to rinse out all of the shampoo with clean water. Use a mane and tail conditioner on his tail after you have washed it. Avoid spraying these products on his face as they can irritate the mucous membranes. When washing his mane be aware that some ponies do not like water near their head and may become agitated. If the pony is very wet use a sweat scraper to remove excess water and prevent him getting chilled.

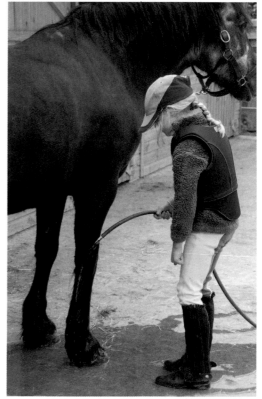

Use a hose to wash off muddy legs.

6.3 CLIPPING

Clipping involves removing either all, or some, of the pony's thick winter coat to prevent him becoming too hot when being worked. There are several types of clip – which one you choose will depend on the type or breed of the pony, his living conditions and his workload.

A thick winter coat can be clipped to prevent the pony sweating when in work and also to make it easier to keep him clean.

We advise you to pay a professional to do this, who will also advise you on the type of clip. Once the pony is clipped he must be appropriately rugged (see Chapter 15).

6.4 PULLING

The term pulling refers to a technique used to shorten the pony's mane and keep the tail neat by pulling the hair out at the root. (Traditionally, mountain and moorland breeds are left with full mane and tail.) Some ponies find this extremely uncomfortable so you may need to use a product which cuts rather than pulls out the hair.

Comb or brush out the mane and tail to remove mud and tangles. Avoid spraying on any conditioner as this will make the hair slippery.

Step 1. Take a small amount of hair between thumb and forefinger and backcomb the remainder so that you have a few longer hairs that can be wrapped around the comb.

Step 2. Tug the comb firmly, which will remove the hair from the root.

Step 3. Repeat this process until the mane is the required length.

Step 4. For the best result regularly brush out the back-combed section so you can see how long the mane is and whether there are any uneven lengths of hair.

Step 5. When pulling the tail only remove the hair from the side and underneath. You will not be able to plait a tail that has been pulled.

Right above: To pull a mane, first backcomb a small amount of hair.

Right below: Wrap the hair around the comb and give a sharp, upward tug to remove the hair.

6.5 TRIMMING

To achieve a neat, uniform finish when trimming the pony's heels use round-ended scissors and a comb. (As with pulling, the mountain and moorland breeds are traditionally left untrimmed.)

First, comb out the hair, then once the comb is between the root of the hair and the tip, use the scissors to trim to the comb.

Always use a comb and blunt-ended scissors when trimming feathers.

Trim the long hairs under the pony's chin and jaw, but do not cut his whiskers. We also advise that you do not cut any hair in or around his ears.

Tails always look neater if the cut edge is straight. Brush the tail out and place your forearm under the pony's dock to judge the length. Ideally the tail should fall approximately 10cm (4in) below the pony's hocks. Hold the tail in one hand fairly close to the bottom and cut it straight across.

Before you trim his tail place your forearm underneath the tail to gauge the correct length.

When trimming the tail always cut away from yourself and the pony.

6.6 PLAITING

It is traditional to plait the pony's mane and tail when he goes to a show or Pony Club event (unless he is a mountain and moorland breed). It is considered correct to have an uneven number of individual plaits along his crest. You can either use a needle and thread or elastic bands to secure the plaits. You will thus need a needle and thread, bands, scissors and a comb.

- Comb the mane and divide into even-sized bunches, securing each one with a band.

- Start from the poll (ears) and work down the neck. The plaits will be easier to secure and are more likely to stay in place if they are tight.

- Stitch around the bottom of each plait and fold it under itself and then under again. Bring the needle and thread up through the middle of the plait, pulling it tight. Wind the thread around the plait and sew through it several times to secure. Cut off the thread close to the hair so that the ends are not visible.

- If you are using plaiting bands, brush out the individual bunch and plait the hair tightly. Secure the end of the plait with a band.

Fold the plait in half and half again, making a neat bundle, which you secure with an additional band.

- Plait the pony's tail as you would a French braid. Taking hair from the very top and sides of the tail, plait until you reach the end of the dock (the bone in the tail). Fold the end of the plait under itself and secure with either thread or a band.

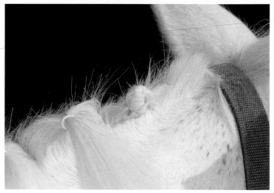

Top left: To ensure that each plait is the same size, divide the mane into bunches and secure each one with a band.

Top right: Making the plaits as tight as possible will help them to stay in place.

Lower left: Secure the bottom of the plait with either a band (as shown) or with a needle and thread.

Lower right: Fold the plait in half and then half again, making a neat bundle and then secure with a band (as shown) or with the thread.

7

DAILY ROUTINE

A well-put-together daily regime for your pony will incorporate a realistic time frame and prioritise welfare. Whether your pony is kept at grass or a combination of stable and turnout, you will need to check him twice a day. A well-managed pony who is settled in an established routine will be easier to handle, amenable to ride and more likely to remain sound.

7.1 THE STABLE-KEPT PONY

The following notes will help you establish a suitable regime for a stable-kept pony.

Daily health checks

When you check your pony, observe whether there is anything about his behaviour that is not usual. For example, is he particularly lethargic or abnormally animated, or is he sweating excessively and obviously distressed? You should also note the state of his bedding, the quantity and condition of droppings, the amount of water he has consumed

Your pony will need to wear an appropriate rug for the weather condition, especially if he is clipped.

and whether he has eaten his hay and hard feed. All of these factors are indicators of the pony's health and well-being (see Chapter 11).

Remove the pony's rugs (if applicable) and run your hands all over him, paying particular attention to his head and legs. You are looking for any cuts, lumps or areas of discomfort (see Chapter 13).

Pick out his feet, looking at the condition of his shoes (see Chapter 10) and contact your farrier if you have any concerns.

If the pony suffers from skin irritations – caused either by insects, the weather or rugs – we advise you to seek veterinary advice as treatment is highly dependent on the root cause of the condition.

Regular grooming (as explained in Chapter 6) helps maintain the condition and health of the pony's coat, and provides a further opportunity to check for cuts, abrasions and swellings.

Regular grooming will help to maintain the condition and health of the pony's coat.

Mucking out

In order for your pony to remain healthy his stable must be kept clean. If your pony is in for long periods you should muck him out thoroughly in the morning and evening. Start by removing all droppings and wet bedding. Place the clean bedding in one corner of the box and sweep the floor thoroughly.

Traditionally, a straw bed will be deep, with substantial banks round the walls. You will not need such a deep bed with high banks if you are using wood shavings. Some forms of bedding and its management work by removing the droppings daily but only taking out the wet every 3–4 days (see table on page 83). Once you have re-laid the pony's bed you will need to skip out (remove droppings) throughout the day.

Ideally, when you are mucking out you should tie the pony in a safe place outside the stable. If you have to keep him in the box you must tie him up so that he cannot injure himself on the tools.

Routinely check the stable for general wear and tear and any damage the pony may have caused.

Straw is traditionally used as bedding, but greedy ponies may eat it.

Store all yard tools neatly and in a safe place where the pony cannot get caught up in them.

Top left: Shavings provide good bedding and droppings must be removed regularly to keep bedding fresh.

Top right: Bedding can be banked up against the walls to prevent draughts.

Lower left: Once the bed has been mucked out thoroughly, you will need to skip any further droppings out, into a bucket, regularly.

Lower right: Sweep the bed back once it has been mucked out and re-laid.

Types of bedding

Traditionally stables had stone floors and bedding was essential to provide comfort and insulation. Nowadays rubber matting is often used on floors as it is warm, durable and provides grip. While the initial outlay is expensive, rubber matting is cost-effective because you are able to use less bedding than for a concrete floor. The type of bedding you use will depend on your pony's health requirements, budget, availability and yard policy.

Bedding	Pros	Cons
Wood shavings	Widely available, biodegradable, absorbent, spore free	Price fluctuates, can irritate skin, sticks to rugs and bandages
Cubed cardboard	Dust/spore free, warm, absorbent, biodegradable	Not widely available, costly
Straw	Widely available, drains rather than absorbs, cost-efficient	Dusty, contains spores, ponies may eat it, can irritate skin, fluctuating quality, needs to be stored under cover
Hemp (Auboise)	Dust/spore free, absorbent, widely available, biodegradable	Costly, but you can reduce costs by removing droppings daily and only taking out wet bedding every three or four days
Paper (shredded)	Warm, dust free, absorbent, biodegradable	Expensive, difficult to obtain

Feeding and watering

If the pony is not going out in the paddock he will need fresh hay. A pony who is stabled for long periods will require his hay ration to be spread out throughout the day in order to mirror his natural feeding pattern.

Top left: Hay is often fed in a haynet.

Top right: In the stable the haynet should be hung from a sturdy ring.

Below left: Secure the haynet with a quick-release knot.

Below right: The net needs to be hung at a height that will prevent the pony getting a foot caught up in it.

The haynet can also be secured to a piece of baler twine to allow a breakage point if he should get himself caught up in the net – this can happen when the hay is eaten and the net hangs much lower in the stable area.

All feed bowls and utensils should be washed after use. Remember it is important to feed at roughly the same time every day.

Watering: scrub out water buckets and refill. If the stable has an automatic drinker, check that it is working and clean it as necessary.

It is important to keep all equipment as clean as possible.

Turnout

Ponies are happier and calmer when they have regular access to turnout. Ideally your pony should spend some part of his day at grass. How much time and when he is out will depend upon yard policy (if applicable), the pony's susceptibility to conditions such as laminitis, sweet itch and sunburn, the time of year and ground conditions. It is common practice for ponies to be turned out overnight during the summer months and during the day in the winter.

Weather permitting, ponies can be turned out without a rug.

7.2 THE GRASS-KEPT PONY

As for a stable-kept pony, it is essential to establish a daily routine for a pony kept at grass.

Catching, grooming and feeding

Ideally, you will be able bring the pony into a fenced area with hard standing where you will be able to handle him safely. If this is not possible you can tie him to a piece of string on a fence line. Do not tie him up to a gate. Check his rug (if worn) for rips or broken straps and remove it, making sure it is out of the way of the pony. Run your hands all over the pony, paying particular attention to the state of his shoes and areas that may have been rubbed by the rug. If your paddock is some distance away from the yard, take a spare rug with you in case you have to replace it.

Grooming. Pick out his feet. Use a dandy brush (see Chapter 6) to remove any dried mud, scurf and loose hair from his body. Brush his head and face with a body brush. Avoid excess brushing and bathing,

Picking out the feet cleans them of debris and gives you a chance to check the state of the shoes.

Ponies love to roll.

which will remove grease from the coat as it reduces its natural ability to repel water and provide warmth. However, washing small areas of his coat as well as his mane and tail will keep him presentable.

Feeding. The safest and most practical way to feed hay is to place it on the ground. To avoid fighting amongst field companions, there should always be one more pile than there are ponies. If your pony lives out

If your pony is out in the snow you will need to provide hay in the paddock.

in company, bring him in to give him his hard feed rather than taking the bucket into the field.

Field checks and grazing management

Walk the perimeter of the paddock, checking the fence line and gate for damage and checking that the water supply is clean and the automatic water trough (if applicable) is in working order.

Remove litter and check for any holes into which your pony could put his foot. If there is a man-made shelter you will need to check for any damage.

Throughout the year, but particularly in the spring and summer months, you need to look out for poisonous plants. Remove ragwort with a specially designed fork, which will pull out the deep roots. It is more potent when dried and therefore must either be burned or put in a dustbin. Ragwort is also toxic to humans, so wear rubber gloves if you are removing it by hand (see Chapter 4).

Remove droppings from the paddock on a daily basis to help reduce the worm burden.

Regularly removing the droppings will help to manage the worm burden and improve the general quality of pasture (see Chapter 4). If you need to restrict the amount of grazing your pony has in the summer months you can use a technique called strip grazing. If you

Strip grazing is an efficient way of limiting the amount of fresh grass available. This is particularly relevant for ponies who have a tendency to carry too much weight during the spring and summer months.

are at a livery yard this will need to be with the consent of the manager. Use electric tape and posts to increase the size of his paddock by a small amount every few days.

Keep safe

- To avoid stacks of bales (of bedding and hay) becoming unsafe, use those from the top of the pile first. (However products such as haylage, that may have a 'use by' date, should be stored in a logical manner, so that newer supplies are not stacked on top of old).

- Store equipment and utensils out of the way of the pony to avoid injury.

- When carrying water, carry a bucket in each hand, which will balance you and avoid unnecessary strain on your back.

- When moving bedding/feed bags/hay bales use a wheelbarrow or sack truck.

Time-saving tips

- Fill haynets in advance and stack neatly.

- Removing droppings from the paddock daily will prevent a labour-intensive build-up and help minimise worm burden.

- Organise tasks in a logical order to minimise the time you travel backwards and forwards across the yard.

- Pick out feet into a skip bucket to avoid unnecessary sweeping.

8

Feeding and Watering

Ponies are nomadic, grazing animals and should, as far as possible, have a regime that closely mirrors their natural feeding pattern. Understanding how, what and why to feed will enable you to create a balance which will benefit your pony's digestive system while maintaining his optimum weight and his overall condition. We explain the importance of forage, the different types available, how best to feed it and when it may be necessary to supplement his diet.

8.1 PRINCIPLES OF FEEDING

The following factors should be taken into consideration when compiling a pony's feeding regime:

Temperament	Weight
Type	Time of year
Work	Existing medical conditions
Age	

A highly nutritious diet – one which includes rich forage and concentrates – is not suitable for ponies who have certain medical conditions (e.g. laminitis – see Chapter 12), are predisposed to put on weight (native breeds) and those who do little work. It may also have an adverse affect on some ponies, making them difficult to ride and handle. However if the pony is older, struggles to keep condition or is expected to work more intensively he may benefit from a diet that is more nutritious. Grass will be high in natural sugars during the spring and autumn and grazing may well need to be restricted. A pony who is predominantly living out will need additional forage during the winter.

As general principles, the following should be observed.

- Feed little and often: this mirrors a pony's natural feeding pattern.

- Feed in a routine: ponies are creatures of habit and thrive on a routine.

Include succulents such as carrots and apples in the daily feed ration.

- Make all changes to feed gradually. This is extremely important as it allows the bacteria in the digestive system to adjust to different food types so that they are broken down effectively. Failure to do so may increase the pony's chances of getting colic.

- Include succulents such as apples and carrots in the diet: these will make the feed more palatable but should be used sparingly as they are high in natural sugars.

- Water before feeding. Generally, water should be available at all times but there are some circumstances – for example, travelling or during periods of exercise – where a pony has not had recent access to water, which can result in mild dehydration. It is important that a pony is rehydrated before he consumes his hard feed to reduce the risk of colic.

- Buy the best quality feed you can afford.

- Fibre (hay/haylage/grass) should constitute the largest component of the total feed ration: because of the composition of the pony's digestive tract, fibre is essential to maintain healthy gut function.

- Hard feed should not be given either an hour before or after exercise: the circulatory system prioritises blood flow to the muscle masses during exercise and cooling down and thus away from the digestive tract. This slows digestion and therefore may increase the likelihood of colic.

How much does he need?

A maintenance ration is the total amount of food a pony who is doing light or no work requires in a 24-hour period to maintain his digestive health, his weight and overall condition. In most cases, your pony will be sustained adequately on forage alone. If the pony's workload demands it, you can replace between 10–15 per cent of his overall ration with a concentrate feed.

Calculating a daily ration

Height in hands (approx)	Bodyweight kg (approx)	Daily ration kg
11hh	200	5
12hh	260	6.5
13hh	320	8
14hh	390	9.75
15hh	490	12.25

The calculation used is: bodyweight in kg divided by 100 × 2.5.

8.2 FORAGE

A pony's digestive system requires a continuous intake of small amounts of fibre of a low nutritional value. Ponies who are paddock-kept and in light work will largely have this fibre provided by grazing. Your pony will need to be given hay/haylage if he is kept in a stable, is in hard work, or during the winter months when grazing is sparse.

Hay and haylage

Hay is made from cut grass that has been allowed to dry naturally before baling. Hay has a lower nutritional value than grass and haylage and, when stored correctly, will remain fresh for a relatively long time. Good-quality hay will be dry, largely free from dust, mould and weeds and have a sweet smell. Hay which contains dust and mould spores may cause respiratory problems.

Haylage is baled before the cut grass is fully dried, retaining up to 50 per cent of its moisture content, and is shrink-wrapped to prevent rotting and to encourage a controlled amount of fermentation. Haylage should be free from mould and debris, have a distinctive smell and break apart easily once opened. Take care when feeding haylage to ponies as its nutritional value is higher than that of grass because of the fermentation of the sugars. It is also more expensive than hay and, once opened, has a relatively short shelf-life.

Hay and haylage should be stored under cover and if possible on pallets. Keep the area as clean as possible, regularly removing old hay and debris. Newly cut green hay which is stacked too tightly and in large quantities may actually become warm and could combust.

How to feed hay/haylage

Having calculated a forage ration for the pony it is best to divide it into smaller portions which are then fed throughout the day. It is most natural for a pony to eat off the ground, however hay supplied in this

way is more likely to be wasted as it will get trampled on and soiled. Other feeding options are:

Hay ball – made from flexible PVC curved bars that will release under pressure. The advantage of the ball is that is can be suspended at a low level allowing the pony to eat in a natural position. In our opinion this is the best feeding solution.

Haynet – should be tied using a quick-release knot and hung at a height that is roughly at the pony's eye level. This will prevent him getting his foot trapped. Note that a child may find it hard to hang a haynet sufficiently high off the floor.

Mangers – there are a number of designs available on the market. They can be expensive but they are easy to fill.

Soaking hay

Dust and spores become sticky when wet, thereby attaching themselves to the hay and passing into the pony's digestive system rather than being inhaled and entering the respiratory

Above left: Good-quality hay will have a sweet smell.

Above centre: Haylage is a highly nutritious forage.

Above right: It can be more economical to buy haylage in large quantities.

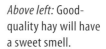

Hay balls are an alternative to a haynet and allow the pony to eat in a more natural position.

tract. Soaking hay will also reduce its nutritional content, which may be necessary if, for example, the pony suffers from laminitis (see Chapter 12). If the hay needs to be soaked *in order to make it more palatable* then it should not be used.

Soak the hay for between 20 minutes and an hour in clean water. If possible use a large vessel that has a plug so that it can be easily drained. Hang the net up to drain off the excess water and use within 12 hours (sooner, in hot weather) to avoid the hay rotting.

8.3 CONCENTRATE FEED

The term is broadly used to describe all feeds other than forage and additives. A traditional method of feeding was to feed 'straights', a term used when the ration was made up from cereals such as oats, barley and maize. Such a ration was more applicable to horses in hard work than to ponies – being too 'rich' for most of the latter. Nowadays it is more common to use a compound feed (see below) for most horses and ponies. Even so, concentrates are not necessarily an essential part of the diet and should be used only if the pony's workload, condition and lifestyle require them. All concentrates should be kept in bins (a dustbin with a well-fitting lid is perfectly adequate). This will keep food fresh and help to reduce the number of vermin.

The types of concentrate most likely to be suitable for ponies are as follows.

Compound feeds. The most economical and simplest way to feed concentrates is to use a compound feed which has been formulated with the appropriate levels of energy, protein, fibre, vitamins and minerals. There are feeds on the market to suit every type and temperament.

Sugar beet. This is high in digestible fibre and provides a low amount of energy. It is palatable and helps to maintain weight, so is often used for elderly ponies or fussy eaters. Sugar beet must always be soaked

Top left: A coarse mix includes appropriate levels of energy, protein, fibre, vitamin and minerals.

Top right: Nuts are an economical and simple way to feed concentrates to your pony.

Lower left: Sugar beet is high in digestible fibre and low in energy.

Lower right: Sugar beet must be soaked before use.

before being fed. Follow manufacturer's instructions for use. Soaked sugar beet cannot be kept for more than 48 hours (less in hot weather) as it will start to ferment.

Chaff is a type of forage (essentially chopped hay) but we have included it in this section as it is generally fed as part of a hard feed. Adding chaff to the pony's feed will help to slow his rate of eating. There are many different types available; however, it is probably best to use one which does not include molasses or oil.

Right: Although chaff is a type of forage it is fed as part of a hard feed.

8.4 SUPPLEMENTS

There is a wide range of supplements on the market – however, if the pony receives a balanced feed ration he should not need anything more in his diet. In some cases your vet or farrier may recommend a specific supplement and a salt or mineral lick may be used.

8.5 FEEDING THE OLDER PONY

As a pony gets older he will probably require a diet that is higher in nutrition and easily digestible. Elderly ponies are likely to have worn teeth and may also suffer from some form of arthritis in the jaw. Both of these factors will result in a pony not being able to grind his food properly and therefore he will not receive the full dietary benefits. Older ponies are also more likely to lose condition in cold weather. To make up this nutritional shortfall you can feed a specially formulated concentrate. To encourage the pony to eat, ensure that the feed is highly palatable.

Measure your pony regularly using a weight tape.

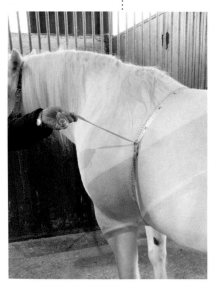

8.6 A HEALTHY WEIGHT

Once you have established how much your pony needs to eat in a day you must be careful not to feed above this amount. If the pony is not thriving on his ration you increase the nutritional value rather than the volume. Overfeeding will result in the pony gaining weight, which may lead to a number of health issues. An obese pony is as much a welfare issue as an emaciated one.

Ponies, especially native breeds, will have a tendency to carry excess bodyweight. Measure your pony's weight regularly using a specially designed tape or a weighbridge. By keeping a record you will be able to create a feeding/exercise regime that is most beneficial to him. A mature pony can be more susceptible to gaining some weight during the summer and losing condition during the winter months, but neither gain nor loss should be extreme.

Approximate bodyweights are shown in the calculating a daily ration table earlier in this chapter.

8.7 WATERING

Ponies need constant access to a clean, fresh water supply in order to survive and thrive. The best way to provide this in a stable is to use either an automatic drinker or buckets. Drinkers are labour-saving and will ensure that your pony is never without water. However, they are liable to freeze in the winter and can easily be damaged. They should be cleaned regularly. Buckets should be sturdy so they cannot be knocked over and will need to be refilled twice a day and scrubbed out daily.

The most efficient way to provide water in a field (see Chapter 4) is to use an automatic water trough, which must be checked daily and cleaned out regularly. Buckets are not advisable in a field as they are easily knocked over. Ponies who only have access to sandy-bottom streams or stagnant ponds may be at risk from colic, and possibly other challenges to their health.

Ponies should have access to a constant supply of clean, fresh water.

9

Maintenance Checks

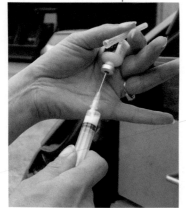

Ponies are routinely vaccinated against tetanus and equine influenza.

As a responsible owner you must ensure that your pony is vaccinated and is on a suitable worming programme. An annual dental check-up is essential for the pony to remain in good health.

9.1 VACCINATIONS

Your pony must be vaccinated against tetanus and equine influenza. Presuming his vaccinations are up to date when you buy him he will only need to be seen annually by the vet to receive his flu booster. The vet will advise how often he will need his tetanus jab. The vet will record this information in your pony's passport.

9.2 WORMING

Ponies naturally harbour a number of internal parasites (known as a worm burden) and must be wormed regularly to reduce them. Allowing these parasites to multiply unchecked can cause significant health problems including colic, lung damage and anaemia. Common

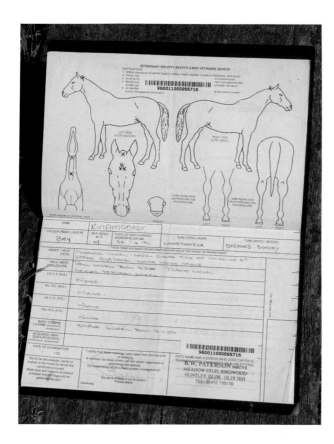

Vaccination records are written up and signed by the vet in the pony's passport.

symptoms of a pony suffering from a heavy worm infestation are a pot belly, loose droppings and a loss of condition and energy.

Worming programme

If your pony is kept on a livery yard it is likely that there will be a programme in place which you will be expected to follow.

Pharmaceutical companies which manufacture wormers have pre-formulated worming programmes available to download. Broadly speaking you worm throughout the year at intervals of 8–13 weeks (depending on the product and manufacturer's guidelines). Twice a year, in the spring and autumn, the pony must be wormed with a product which is specifically formulated to eradicate tapeworm.

For advice on worming, speak to your vet.

Worm count

Faecal egg counts may be carried out four times a year and can estimate the level of infestation and types of larvae present. Veterinary practices may offer this service and it may form part of a livery yard's approach to formulating a programme. A worm count assists in targeting the relevant parasites and worming only when necessary.

Worming products can be added to your pony's feed.

How to worm

Your pony can receive his worming dose either by oral syringe or have it added to his feed. It is advisable that for a period of time (refer to manufacturer's guidelines) your pony remains either in his stable or on a restricted grazing area so that droppings can be removed. Again, this practice may be a feature of a livery yard's strategy.

9.3 TEETH

A pony's teeth continually grow (erupt) throughout his life. The action of grinding vegetation may lead to uneven wear of the teeth. Any sharp surfaces and hooks will cause ulcerations and discomfort when the pony eats, or wears his bridle. If your pony drops quantities of chewed food out of his mouth (known as quidding) he will quickly lose condition and risks developing colic. Your pony should be seen regularly by either an equine dentist or a vet who will file down the teeth leaving smooth, rounded edges. Older ponies will require particular attention as they may have loose or displaced teeth.

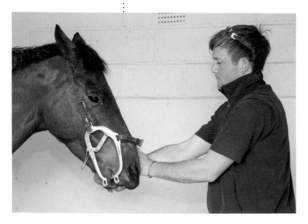

An equine dentist (or vet) will keep your pony's teeth in good order.

Mouth conformation

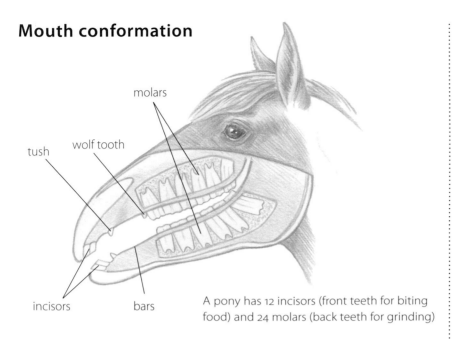

molars

wolf tooth

tush

incisors

bars

A pony has 12 incisors (front teeth for biting food) and 24 molars (back teeth for grinding)

Common dental problems

Wolf teeth. Some ponies may have wolf teeth. These small, under-developed teeth are located near the bars of the mouth. If they cause problems with bitting they can be removed by a vet.

Retained caps. Ponies are born with milk caps on their teeth and as the pony matures the caps fall off naturally, revealing their adult teeth. In some cases a pony will 'retain a cap'. This will have to be removed by a vet to prevent any risk of infection.

Displaced/missing teeth. Missing teeth will create gaps in the mouth where food can become lodged and cause infection and gum irritation. This is particularly prevalent in the older pony.

Tooth abscess. An abscess will cause excessive salivation and extreme discomfort. Often symptoms are a bad-smelling mouth and signs of discomfort when eating or being ridden. You must seek immediate veterinary advice.

10

Foot and Shoeing

The old adage 'no foot no horse' is a relevant one. Put simply, a pony with good foot conformation is far more likely to stay sound. There is much written about this complex topic – however, we aim to give you a working knowledge of the basics. Meticulous care should be taken in order to maintain the pony's feet in the best possible condition. For this reason we outline the basic structure of a foot and detail a daily care routine. We touch on the link between diet and the health of the feet and explain shoeing and trimming.

10.1 FOOT CONFORMATION AND STRUCTURE

Foot conformation will substantially dictate the pony's long-term soundness, his resale value, his insurance cover and crucially his ability to carry out the job you have planned for him. Broadly speaking, a pony should have two pairs of feet, namely a symmetrical hind pair and fore pair. This symmetry allows his weight to be borne evenly, thus reducing uneven stress on the structures. In addition the feet should be a good shape, with the forefeet being slightly rounder than their squarer hind counterparts.

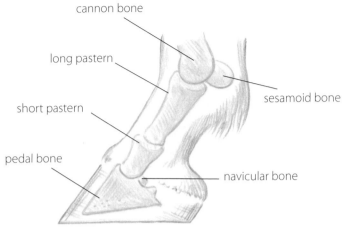

cannon bone

long pastern

short pastern

pedal bone

sesamoid bone

navicular bone

Left: The drawing shows a cross-section through the fetlock, pasterns and hoof. *below:* The drawing shows the underside of the foot.

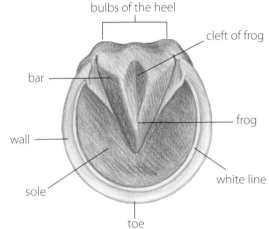

bulbs of the heel

cleft of frog

bar

frog

wall

white line

sole

toe

Below: For a pony to move comfortably and efficiently, it is important that his feet are kept 'balanced' by appropriate attention from the farrier. A good hoof/pastern axis (*below left*) is achieved when there is a continuous line down the front of his pasterns and hoof, that is parallel to the midline angle of the pasterns. From the front (*below right*) the sole of the foot should sit level on the ground, and both sides of the lower limb should look equal, either side of a plumb-line vertically down the centre of the limb.

side view

front view

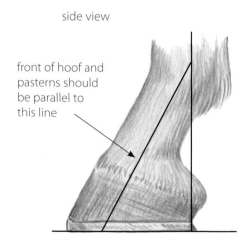

front of hoof and pasterns should be parallel to this line

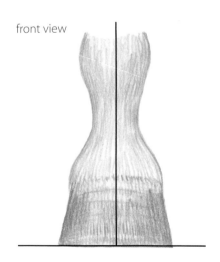

10.2 FOOT CARE

The majority of foot problems arise because of a general lack of care, such as not picking out the feet regularly, leaving too long a time between visits by the farrier, and a poorly managed diet.

The way the feet are conformed leaves them vulnerable to bruising and it is for this reason that the pony's feet must be picked out twice daily to remove mud and stones. Starting at the heel, use the hoof pick in a downward direction towards the toe, taking care not to damage the triangular structure in the centre of hoof know as the frog. Clean the grooves either side of the frog and then the sole of the foot. If the pony is shod, a lost, loose or twisted shoe will require immediate attention from the farrier.

Take care not to damage the frog or bulbs of the heel when picking out a hoof.

A healthy hoof will not smell unless the pony has developed a condition known as thrush (see Chapter 12). Ponies who are stabled for long periods can develop thrush as soiled bedding packs in the feet, providing the ideal environment for bacteria and other micro-organisms.

The hoof wall and the sole of the foot should be firm and have an even texture. Any deterioration in quality may result in areas that are flaky, crumbly or slightly spongy. This may be caused by prolonged exposure to waterlogged paddocks or poorly drained stabling. Poor horn quality may also be linked to diet: either to a deficiency or an excess of certain vitamins and minerals. Some ponies, however, may simply have a predisposition to poor horn quality. Consult your farrier or your vet who will be able to advise you on both the cause and the course of action. They may suggest the use of a relevant feed supplement. There are a variety of oils and balms that claim to improve the quality of equine hooves. In our opinion these will not make a significant difference but will add the finishing touch to a well-turned out pony.

A pony who consumes an excessive amount of carbohydrates in his diet will be susceptible to developing a condition known as laminitis (see Chapter 12). This is a serious condition that causes inflammation of the sensitive laminae in the feet and often affects ponies who are carrying too much weight. If the pony has a history of laminitis he will need to be managed carefully in order to prevent recurrent bouts of the condition.

Picking up feet for cleaning and inspection

This needs to be done in a way that is clear and comfortable for the pony and safe for the handler.

Picking up a forelimb

Stand at the pony's left shoulder and face his tail. Run your hand down the back of his leg, starting at the back of the knee. When you reach the fetlock place your hand around the joint and tug gently upwards while, at the same time, applying some pressure with your bodyweight against his side. This will encourage the pony to lift his foot. Bring your hand round the limb so that your palm rests on the front of the hoof, providing support. Always hold the hoof rather than the leg.

When picking out a foot, hold the hoof rather than the leg to provide support.

Picking up a hind limb

Put your hand on the pony's withers and run your hand the length of his back, moving predictably along his body until you are standing by his hip. Making sure the pony knows you are there, run your hand down the front of his hind leg below the hock (cannon bone) finishing with your hand on the front of his hind hoof and your thumb at the back of the pastern. Tug gently upwards while applying pressure against his body to encourage him to lift his foot (see photo on page 72).

10.3 SHEOING AND TRIMMING

Shoeing a pony will provide him with grip and protect his feet from excessive wear on hard surfaces. A skilled farrier will also be able to correct, or at least improve, some conformational defects.

Right: Your pony should be seen by the farrier every six to eight weeks.

Below left: A skilled farrier may be able to improve some conformational defects.

Below right: A well-shod hoof provides both grip and support.

Your pony will need to see a farrier every six to eight weeks. If he is unshod he will still require regular trimming in order to keep his feet in good shape and in correct balance. Whether your pony is able to be unshod will depend on the conformation of his feet, the quality of the hoof and his workload. In some cases ponies are shod only in front,

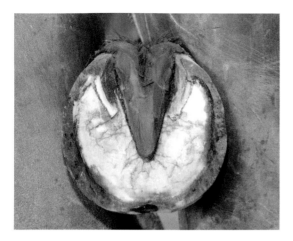 

which will reduce the risk of injury from kicking. This is particularly relevant if your pony is turned out in a large group.

How to recognise when the pony needs re-shoeing

The first indication that your pony needs shoeing is that the clenches have risen. A clench is the term used for the nails that fix the shoe to the hoof. The tips of these nails are driven through the hoof wall and then bent down to secure the shoe. As the hoof grows the clenches are pulled and they will start to become more prominent and feel raised. You will be able to feel this by running your hand around the hoof wall. Because of the constant nature of the hoof growth there will be occasions when the hoof begins to grow over the shoe. If the pony is worked regularly on hard surfaces the shoes will become worn and lose their grip. A loose shoe will make a distinct sound when it comes into contact with a hard surface. If the pony has a twisted shoe you need to phone a farrier immediately. You should not let your child ride their pony if he is missing a shoe.

Above left: A trimmed and balanced hoof prior to being shod.

Above right: A well-shod foot.

11

Pony's Health

The first indication that your pony might be unwell will be a change in his usual behaviour and demeanour. It is important to recognise what is normal for your pony and to be able to identify the signs of good health. We explain how to check your pony's temperature, pulse and respiration and the principles of sick nursing.

11.1 SIGNS OF GOOD HEALTH

As you get to know your pony your ability to recognise when he is not well will become second nature. You may not know *what* is wrong, but you will know that *something* is. It is always sensible to err on the side of caution and contact your vet if you have any concerns about your pony's health. If your pony is kept in a stable, check to see whether his bed is more disturbed than usual. This could indicate that he has been either pacing or rolling excessively. Note whether he seems either abnormally restless or lethargic. In the field a pony who is unwell or distressed may withdraw from the group and stand alone. He might also spend more time lying down than usual, or stand in an abnormal way such as pointing one forefoot forwards or in rocking position trying to take the weight off his forefeet.

A healthy pony should:

- Be alert and interested in what's going on around him.

- Have a shiny coat with no signs of sweating.

- Be breathing regularly with no obvious signs of distress.

- Have no discharge from either his eyes or his nose.

- Bear weight on all four limbs.

- Have no swelling or heat in his legs.

- Have normal droppings – firm and round – and the usual amount, and his urine should not smell excessively or be dark in colour.

- Be eating and drinking normally.

Above: A healthy pony should be alert and interested in his surroundings.

Left: A pony who is unwell may withdraw from the group and stand on his own.

11.2 VITAL SIGNS

Keeping a record of your pony's temperature, pulse and respiration will help you to monitor his health and alert you to any possible illness.

Temperature

A healthy pony will have a core body temperature of around 38 °C (100.5 °F). Keep a record of his resting core temperature as a sudden rise may indicate an infection. Equally significant is any drop below his core temperature, which is usually associated with hypothermia and blood loss.

Stand at the side of the pony to insert a thermometer into his rectum.

To take the temperature

You will need a digital thermometer and petroleum jelly.

Grease the thermometer with petroleum jelly.

Standing to one side of the pony, lift his tail.

Hold the thermometer firmly and gently insert it into his rectum.

Push it to one side so that you are taking the temperature of the rectal wall.

Remove the thermometer when it beeps. (Not all models do this, in which case wait for about a minute before removing.)

Pulse

A normal resting pulse rate is between 36–42 beats per minute. A raised pulse at rest is a strong indication that the pony is either in pain or suffering from stress. To record his pulse rate accurately take it when he is relaxed and has not worked that day.

To take the pony's pulse manually you will need to press your fingers under the jaw until you find the area where the artery crosses the bone. Maintain the pressure and count the beats for 15 seconds then multiply the number by four which will give you beats per minute. You can also find his pulse (radial) on the inside of his forearm.

Respiration

A pony will have a resting respiration rate of 8 to 12 breaths per minute. A rise in rate may indicate that the pony is working harder than normal to breathe. This often indicates that the respiratory tract has become irritated by a virus, an allergen or bacteria.

To count the breaths per minute, stand a safe distance behind the pony and watch the ribs rise and fall. A rise and fall count as one breath. Alternatively, count the breaths by watching the nostrils – this is easier in winter against the cold air.

Place two fingers under the jaw bone to feel the pony's pulse.

11.3 SICK-NURSING

In some cases it may be necessary to place your pony in quarantine if there is any chance of the infection spreading. If your pony is on a yard there will be procedures in place to deal with this situation. It is sensible to invest in a set of waterproof overalls that you can remove when you leave the yard. Use disinfectant to clean your footwear, hands, grooming kit and any tools. This will help prevent the spread of infection.

A pony who is either ill or injured will need to be carefully looked after so that he recovers as quickly as possible.

If your pony is on box rest ensure he has access to ad lib hay so that his gut can function sufficiently.

- First ensure that you understand all of the vet's instructions and follow them exactly. They may tell you how they expect the pony to respond to treatment. If the pony does not appear to be responding within the specified time you will need to consult your vet.

- When feeding a pony who is on box rest your aim is to maintain his condition, allow any medication that is to be given in the food to be consumed and prevent him from developing any additional conditions associated with diet. Always clean his feed bowl after each use.

- Ensure your pony has ad lib hay (or haylage, if that is what he receives normally). It is important that his gut continues to function. If he is used to grazing continually he may be at risk of colic if he is suddenly confined to a stable.

- If the pony has significant discharge from his nose you should feed small amounts of hay on the ground or in a low-set hay ball. This will avoid a situation where you have to waste hay because it is contaminated.

- If your pony normally lives out and is confined to a stable he will settle better if he can see other horses.

- Make sure that his bed is kept really clean.

- Depending on the weather and the individual pony you may need to rug him to keep him warm.

- Ensure that his water buckets are scrubbed out and replaced regularly.

12

Common Disorders

The disorders outlined in this chapter are those you are most likely to come across. Some of these can be avoided through correct management of your pony.

12.1 CIRCULATORY DISORDERS

Symptoms	Cause(s)	What to do
Azoturia, also referred to as **tying up, setfast** and **EER (equine exertional rhabdomyolysis):** extreme reluctance to move, grinding of teeth, sweating, muscles hard and shaking.	The precise cause of the condition is not clear but there are several factors or triggers. Ponies who are predominantly stabled but are receiving a large ration of hard feed and are doing minimal or no work; a strong genetic predisposition; dehydration and electrolyte imbalance; erratic work pattern.	Don't move the pony. If he is out on a ride you will need to arrange for transport to get him home. Put a rug on him to keep him warm. Do not let him eat. Call the vet.
Lymphangitis: large amount of swelling distorting all aspects of the leg; can affect one or all legs; heat in the leg; swelling will hinder joint's ability to move.	Inflammation of the lymphatic system triggered by erratic feeding patterns, long periods of immobility, or an infected wound.	Contact your vet, who will advise cold hosing, gentle exercise and possibly a course of antibiotics.

12.2 SKIN AND EYE DISORDERS

Symptoms	Cause(s)	What to do
Mud fever: inflammation of skin; broken and scabby skin; can develop a secondary, underlying infection.	Prolonged exposure to wet and muddy conditions; a genetic predisposition, sensitive skin.	Clean the affected area with anti-microbial/surgical wash. Towel dry. Remove any scabs. At this point you might apply an ointment prescribed by the vet.
Rain scald: large patches of scabby skin; hair loss; inflammation. More prevalent on faces, backs, withers.	Prolonged exposure to cold winter weather.	Clean the area with anti-microbial scrub and move the pony to grazing with better shelter and if necessary put a rug on him.
Ringworm: bald patches exposing sore skin.	Fungal infection (can be caught by humans). Extremely contagious by touch.	The pony must be put in quarantine. Contact your vet who will prescribe an anti-fungal treatment. Be aware that stable, tack and all other equipment used for the pony will need to be decontaminated with a relevant solution to prevent re-infection.
Sweet itch: incessant itching leading to bald, sore skin. Most noticeable on manes and tails.	Hypersensitivity to biting insects particularly prevalent during spring, summer and autumn months.	Biting insects are most active at sunrise and sunset. Try to avoid turning out during these periods. In addition it may be necessary to use a sweet itch rug and an effective insect repellent.
Fly bites: swellings and areas of sensitivity.	Biting insects of any type but often horseflies.	If fly bites are excessive or in problem areas you should contact your vet for advice.
Conjunctivitis: inflamed membrane and discharge of the eye.		Use a fly mask to prevent insects transferring the infection to other ponies. Discuss treatment with your vet.

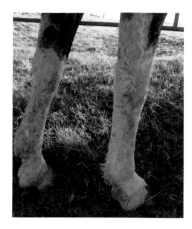

Mud fever can affect large areas of the skin.

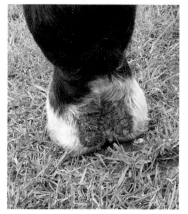

Left untreated, mud fever can lead to secondary infections.

Prolonged exposure to wet, muddy conditions can result in mud fever and other skin conditions.

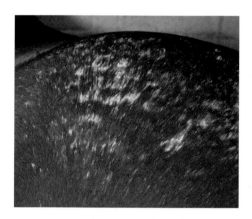

Rain scald can lead to extensive hair loss.

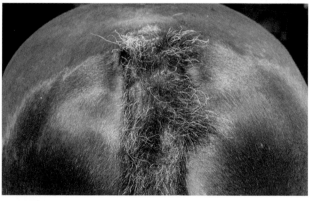

A combination of medical preparations, management and rugs can significantly reduce sweet itch outbreaks.

Sweet itch causes the pony a lot of discomfort if left untreated.

12.3 FOOT DISORDERS

Symptoms	Cause(s)	What to do
Laminitis: lameness affecting all or some of the feet; pony adopting a unusual stance in an attempt to eliminate the pressure from his toes; warm feet; digital pulse; sweating; reluctance to move.	Inflammation of the laminae caused by either excess consumption of carbohydrate (i.e. rich grass), poisoning; a side effect of either equine metabolic syndrome or Cushing's; the result of excessive work on hard ground (concussive laminitis).	Remove your pony from the grass and contact your vet and farrier immediately. It is likely that both these professionals will have an input in your pony's recovery and your management of the condition.
Seedy toe: mild to severe lameness; the hoof is painful when tapped; presence of black pus which may be dry and crumbly.	Ponies who have poor horn quality and a long toe which results in separation at the white line (see drawing of underside of foot in Chapter 10) which harbours infection. A condition which will cause the widening or discolouring of the white line.	This is a condition which most likely will be identified by your farrier, who should shoe the pony accordingly.
Pus in the foot: acute lameness; reluctance to move; warm feet; digital pulse.	An abscess within the hoof capsule.	We advise that you contact your farrier who should be able to drain the abscess and advise you how to proceed.
Thrush: affects the underside of the foot (often the frog); smells; can cause the frog to rot.	Infection often the result of standing in soiled bedding for a prolonged period and poor foot management.	Scrub the foot with antibacterial wash and spray with iodine. Ensure pony's bed is kept clean and his feet are picked out regularly.

Unpleasant smelling hooves with soft, blackened areas are signs of a thrush infection.

12.4 RESPIRATORY DISORDERS

Symptoms	Cause(s)	What to do
Recurrent airway obstruction (RAO): laboured breathing at rest; persistent cough; nasal discharge. In severe cases lethargy and reluctance to work.	An allergy to fungal spores on hay and straw, or possibly pollen.	Turn the pony out as much as possible; use an alternative bedding such as shavings; soak hay or use haylage; contact your vet.
Strangles: high temperature; cough; lack of appetite; nasal discharge. Glands under the jaw bone become swollen and develop into abscesses.	A bacterial infection.	This is extremely contagious and if one horse has it on the yard no horses will be allowed either in or out until the quarantine period (usually 2 weeks from the last case) has expired. Contact your vet who can confirm whether your pony has strangles and advise you further.
Equine viral herpes (EVH1): symptoms include nasal discharge; cough; loss of appetite.	A virus.	If you suspect your pony has recently come into contact with EHV1 contact your vet. It is extremely infectious and the pony will need to be isolated. A vaccine is available.

Nasal discharge can be a symptom of a number of contagious conditions and will require veterinary advice.

12.5 DIGESTIVE DISORDERS

Symptoms	Cause(s)	What to do
Colic: agitated body language including pony kicking at his stomach and grinding his teeth. Sweating and rolling. In some cases droppings will very loose, in others there will be a lack of droppings. Raised pulse; he may be in considerable pain.	Colic can result from an impaction (blockage), twisted gut (strangulated intestine), spasmodic (gas) colic. All of these will present in a similar way and one type of colic can lead to another. For this reason all cases must be treated as potentially serious.	If the pony is out you should bring him in; if he is in a stable remove food and water until you have contacted your vet.
Choke: stretched out neck posture; large quantities of saliva running from the mouth. In some cases partially chewed food matter will come out of the nose. The pony will become progressively more distressed.	Often the cause is related to his teeth; older ponies may have missing or excessively worn teeth, making the effective grinding of food difficult and leading them to try to swallow food that is insufficiently chewed. Younger animals with sharp or displaced teeth will also struggle to grind food adequately. Some ponies 'bolt' their food without chewing it sufficiently.	Move the pony to a quiet area and seek advice from your vet.

13

Equine First Aid

We explain the basic procedures used in dealing with any wound or lameness your pony may have. In many cases first aid is simply what you will need to do prior to the vet arriving. A relatively minor wound may develop into something more serious if not treated correctly. It is for this reason that it is important that you are able to recognise what you can deal with safely and what requires veterinary or other professional assistance.

13.1 BASIC PROCEDURES

When you contact the vet you will need to explain the situation and mention any relevant previous or existing injuries or medical conditions. The more accurate information you can give to the vet the quicker they will be able to assess the situation. If you are able to, bring the pony into an area of hard standing with lighting and access to water. Depending on the weather, and if the pony is suffering from shock, you will need to put a rug on him so that he is kept warm. Check his passport to confirm that the pony has up to date tetanus cover.

Rugging a pony for warmth.

Below: Run your hand down the pony's leg to check for heat, swelling or points of pain.

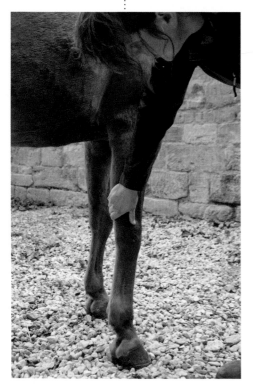

Assessing lameness

In order to gauge the extent of an injury you will need to check over your pony thoroughly. In the first instance carefully pick out his feet. Be aware that he may struggle to transfer the weight from one foot to another. To avoid making the situation worse it is probably best to limit your assessment to whether he is willing to move and bear weight on all four limbs. Avoid turning him tightly or moving him unnecessarily. While carrying out your assessment run your hands (don't wear gloves for this) slowly down all four of his legs. You are looking for heat, swelling and points of pain. As a general guide, warm patches indicate points of injury or infection. Take care when feeling his legs as he may be unusually sensitive, which could make him unpredictable.

First aid for minor injuries

The vet will want to know where the injury is, the depth and size of any wounds and whether there is any bleeding. The most effective way of cleaning a wound is to cold hose the affected area. This will help the blood vessels to contract, which will slow or stop the blood flow, remove any debris out of the wound without further contamination and provide a small amount of pain relief by numbing the area. Do this by using a hosepipe with slow water pressure and direct it so that the water is flowing from just above the wound and running down over it. Hose the area for between 10 and 20 minutes. Do not put anything on the wound as the vet may need to stitch it and will be unable to do so if there is any lotion or spray on the area. Avoid removing anything from the wound as you could make the situation worse. Cold hosing can also help to reduce swelling and minimise discomfort caused by soft tissue injuries and swellings.

Sunburn can be treated by applying a suitable-strength sun block and by reducing the pony's exposure to sunlight.

Cold hosing will help reduce inflammation.

Blood loss

In the case of an arterial or venous bleed, which will result in significant bleeding, you will need to call a vet immediately and apply a pressure bandage (see section 13.2) to the wound to try to stem the bleeding. The combination of the swabs and the bandages allows you to apply pressure to the wound whilst absorbing the blood flow. You may need to use more than one bandage. In more minor cases of blood loss, cold hosing for 5–10 minutes may be enough to stop the bleeding, allowing you to assess the wound.

Puncture wound

Puncture wounds are often underestimated. It is important to realise that while they often present with a small entry wound they can be deceptively deep. Whatever has caused the wound might be visible, but it might be deeper within the wound, making it appear that there is nothing there. Puncture wounds often heal superficially in a short space of time, making them even harder to detect. This can lead to an infection which festers undetected and can result in an abscess, septicaemia or even fatal joint damage. To err on the side of caution it is best to seek veterinary advice if your pony has a puncture wound.

13.2 BANDAGES AND DRESSINGS

For the purpose of first aid and injury treatment you may need to apply either a stable (sometimes called support) bandage or a pressure bandage (used for stemming blood flow). It is also useful know how to use a poultice.

Stable bandages and dressings

Always bandage legs in pairs (both forelimbs and both hind limbs), which will ensure you provide even support, because the limb which is not injured will be bearing more weight than usual. To achieve uniform pressure and tension ideally the same person should bandage both legs. It is important to use under-wraps as padding when using stable bandages (see Chapter 15) to eliminate pressure points. Do not use any type of elasticated bandage (i.e. exercise or tail bandage) for this purpose. When bandaging make sure you have everything you need to hand.

Applying a stable bandage

Step 1. Crouch down by the leg, but at the side, not in front of or behind the pony. Do not kneel or put your hands down on the ground.

Step 2. Take the under-wrap and place round the leg (below the knee or hock), taking care that where the two ends meet is on the outside of the limb, and hold in place with one hand.

Step 3. Bandage from front to back (on the right legs this is clockwise), working your way down the limb applying even pressure. Bandage to just below the fetlock then bandage back up the limb with the bandage finishing just below the knee or the hock and the Velcro fastening on the outside of the limb.

Step 4. To check the pressure of the bandage, place your finger between the pony's leg and the top of the bandage to gauge that the pressure is supportive rather than restrictive.

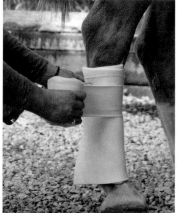
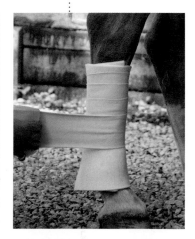

Applying a stable bandage

Top left: Place the under-wrap around the limb.

Top centre: Always bandage from front to back.

Top right: Each wrap of the bandage should be uniform.

Lower left: Apply even pressure as you bandage.

Lower right: Finished stable bandage with Velcro fastening on the outside

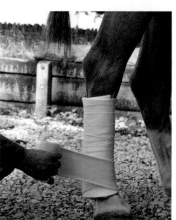
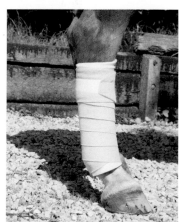

Applying a dressing

Dressings will either come pre-cut or you will need to cut them to the relevant size. Make sure it is a generous size as it may slip when you are bandaging it to the leg.

Step 1. Hold the dressing in place with one hand and then cover with the wrap.

Step 2. Apply a stable bandage as above.

Poultices

Poultices can be applied either wet or dry.

A modern poultice dressing can be used in either a wet or dry state. To use in a wet state you will need to immerse the dressing in boiled water, then drain and leave to cool. Once cooled apply to the wound with the shiny backing uppermost. In its wet state the poultice will provide a moist wound-healing environment as well as drawing out any infection or foreign material. The dressing will need to be replaced every 12 hours – more regularly if the wound is heavily infected. In its dry state this will provide a sterile, absorbent dressing that will not transfer fibres into the wound.

Bandaging a foot

One of the most effective ways of bandaging a foot is to bandage over a clean nappy. This provides enough padding to prevent you inadvertently putting pressure points on the heel and coronary band and goes some way to preventing the pony from walking through the bandage.

Step 1. Pick up the foot.

Step 2. Open up the nappy.

Step 3. Place the toe of the foot in the fold of the nappy.

Step 4. Close the nappy around the foot and secure with the tabs.

Step 5. Use Vetwrap to tape over the nappy to keep it in place.

Applying a pressure bandage

A pressure bandage is primarily used to help stem the flow of blood.

Step 1. Cover the wound with sterile wadding or swabs.

Step 2. Apply a stable bandage over the top to secure the dressing. You may need to use a second swab and then another bandage if the blood continues to soak through.

13.3 FIRST AID KIT

A well-stocked first aid kit should contain the relevant equipment including a selection of uncontaminated scrubs and treatments, all of which should be within their 'use by' date. Make a list of the contents of the kit and paste it on the inside of the first aid box along with the name and number of both the vet and the farrier. This will allow anyone using it to see at a glance exactly what is inside. This is particularly relevant if you are trying to locate an item in an emergency. You will also need to carry a separate first aid kit in your trailer or lorry.

A first aid kit should contain all the relevant equipment – used items should be replaced, and medicines maintained within their 'use by' date.

Contents of a first aid kit

Digital thermometer
Stable bandages (4)
Self-adhesive bandage
Fybergee/leg wraps (4)

Sterile dressings
Swabs

Anti-microbial scrub
Poultice

Latex gloves
Duct tape

Scissors
Antiseptic spray
Small stainless steel dish (to bathe a poultice)
Salt
Wound healing gel

14

Saddlery

For your child to be able to ride their pony safely and effectively they will need a well-fitting saddle and bridle. Your pony may come with tack; however, if this is not the case, remember that what you buy does not need to be new but it must fit the pony correctly, be in good condition and be the correct size for the child. There is a huge range of equipment available so to help you avoid making expensive mistakes we explain exactly what you need to buy in the first instance – you may wish to buy additional items in the future. Your child should be encouraged to learn how to tack up their pony correctly. However, they may require some adult guidance particularly with regard to safety. For this reason we have outlined a step-by-step guide to tacking up and untacking.

14.1 BRIDLES AND BITS

A bridle is generally made of leather and comprises headpiece, cheekpieces, browband, a cavesson noseband, bit and reins. It can be bought as a whole or as individual pieces although we advise that you buy it as a complete item (though in due course you may possibly wish to substitute the items listed below). Generally bridles come in extra full, full, cob, pony and extra small sizes.

Nosebands

The three most widely used nosebands are the cavesson, flash and drop. Complete bridles are most likely to be supplied 'off the shelf' with a cavesson or flash. The former provides little or no action but completes the bridle and can also be used as an anchor point for a standing martingale (see below). The use of a flash noseband or indeed a drop is primarily to keep the pony's mouth closed and prevent him from avoiding the action of the bit whilst being ridden.

Reins

Reins are available in two lengths, namely pony and full. There are a number of types on the market including, plain leather, Continental (half leather/half canvas with leather stops for added grip), rubberised reins (half leather/half rubber-coated canvas) and plaited and laced, both of which have leather detailing for grip and bio-grip. Full-length reins should not be used for children on ponies, since the unnecessarily long loops may pose a safety hazard.

Bits

The bit fits over the pony's tongue and rests on the bars of his mouth. There are several 'families' of bits largely defined by their action (the effect the bit exerts on the pony when in use). However, the most commonly used type of bit (and the one which is the most suitable to be used by an inexperienced rider) is the snaffle. There is a wide range of snaffle bits on the market. If you are unsure as to which is the most relevant bit, or if it becomes apparent that a slighter stronger alternative would be appropriate in certain situations, you should seek advice from either your child's regular riding instructor or a Pony Club coach, who will have the advantage of seeing your child and pony in action.

Bits nowadays are measured in centimetres and the measurement refers to the mouthpiece excluding the bit rings. To check that the bit is the right size for the pony's mouth there should be a small amount of bit visible on both sides of his mouth. A bit that is too wide will slide from side to side when the pony is being ridden. This will not only cause rubbing but will compromise the riders' feel and ability to control the pony. Bits that are too narrow will pinch the pony's cheeks

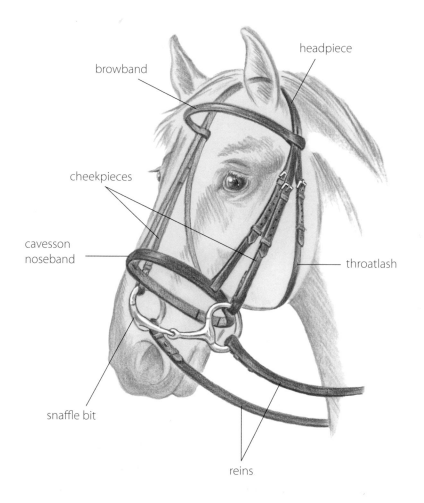

browband

headpiece

cheekpieces

cavesson noseband

throatlash

snaffle bit

reins

This 'see-through' drawing of a pony's head shows the main elements of a bridle. (In real life, the headpiece fits round both ears).

Fulmer snaffle (top); eggbutt snaffle (middle); hanging-cheek snaffle (bottom); loose-ring sweet iron (right).

Continental gag with lozenge mouthpiece (top); pelham with curb chain and lip strap (below).

and lips, causing rubs and discomfort. In addition, a narrow bit can lead to behavioural issues such as head twitching and a reluctance to have the bridle put on.

Martingales

The purpose of a martingale is to prevent the pony from raising his head above the action of the bit, thus compromising rider control. The two most commonly used martingales are the running and the standing. The former works on the reins to create a pulley-like action while

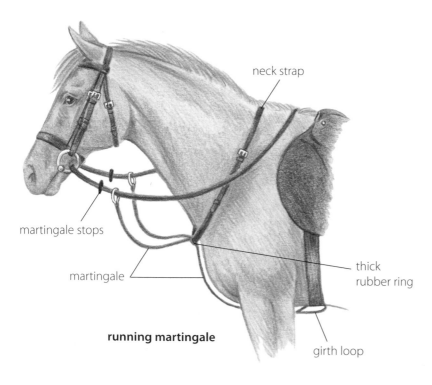

neck strap

martingale stops

martingale

thick
rubber ring

girth loop

running martingale

Running and standing
martingales.

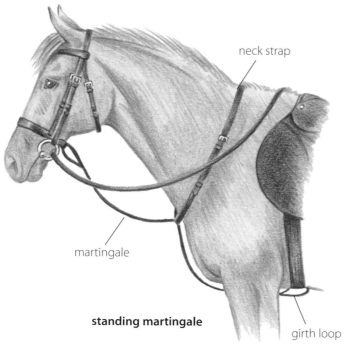

neck strap

martingale

standing martingale

girth loop

the latter is attached directly to the noseband to hold the pony's head carriage at a lower point.

Putting on a running martingale

Step 1. Place the neck strap of the martingale around the pony's neck. Ideally there should be a hand's width (approximately 10–12cm/4–5in) of clearance between his shoulder and the strap. The junction between the broad strap, the neck strap and the two narrower 'ring straps' ideally sits in the centre of his chest and is held together by a rubber bung stop.

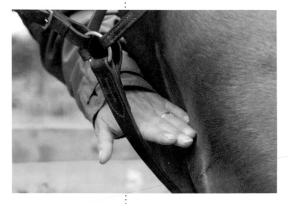

Above left: The martingale strap should sit in the centre of the pony's chest and have a hand's width clearance.

Above right: The martingale straps are held together with a rubber bung stop.

Step 2. Thread the broad strap between the pony's forelegs.

Step 3. Feed the girth though the loop at the end of the strap and secure the saddle as normal.

Step 4. To check whether the ring straps are the correct length for the pony, take them towards his jaw and the rings should roughly reach his throat. If the martingale is adjusted so that it is *too short* it can actually end up being counterproductive.

Step 5. Finally thread a rein through each ring. The reins must have martingale stops, which are made of leather or rubber and sit between the martingale ring and the bit. The purpose of the stops is to prevent the rein buckles and martingale rings becoming tangled, which will lessen the control the rider has and may cause the pony to panic.

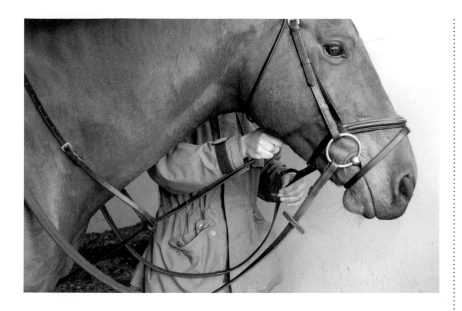

Checking the fit of the ring straps on a standing martingale.

Putting on a standing martingale

This is fitted in the same way as the running martingale but instead of two individual ring straps a standing martingale has one broad strap which attaches directly to the back of a cavesson noseband. Do not attach it to a drop noseband. A correctly fitted standing martingale will have a small amount of play in the broad strap, allowing the pony free movement of his head.

Grass reins

The sole purpose of grass reins is to prevent the pony from putting his head down in an attempt to eat the grass and pulling the reins from the child's hands. There are several designs on the market but the one which we recommend as being the most effective and the simplest to use is a single length of either leather or nylon with a buckle to adjust the length and a rotating clip at either end.

Grass reins prevent the pony from putting his head down to eat the grass when your child is riding.

To fit, attach one end of the grass reins to the saddle ring and the other to the bit and have the clips face outwards. To assess the correct length for the pony, attach one end of the reins to the saddle and adjust the length so that they reach the base of the pony's ears. This will ensure that the grass reins do not exert any pressure on the bit unless the pony drops his head below a certain point.

14.2 SADDLES AND GIRTHS

A poorly fitting saddle can lead to significant behavioural issues as well as causing long-term damage to the pony's back. For these reasons it is crucial that you have the saddle, whether it is new, second-hand or even the one the pony came with, fitted by a professional saddler.

The parts of a general-purpose saddle.

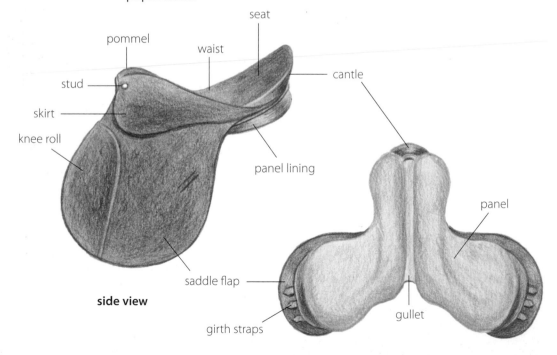

side view

underside

The pony will need a general-purpose saddle (GP), which means it is suitable for all riding disciplines. Saddles can be made from either leather or a synthetic material. A leather one is more traditional and, if cared for properly, more durable. The advantage of a synthetic saddle is that it is lighter and more affordable and some designs can be adjusted by changing the gullet.

Stirrup leathers

Stirrup leathers are available in child and adult lengths and should be used as a pair. When the child has the stirrups at the correct length for them, there should be at least four holes, both above and below the hole you are using, to allow for adjustment.

Stirrup irons

From a safety point of view there must be a finger's width either side of your child's foot when it is in the stirrup. You can put rubber treads in the irons, which will provide grip and help the rider to 'keep their stirrups'. We strongly advise that children use safety irons. These irons will either have an open side with a rubber loop, or a shaped side, which makes it less likely that your child's foot will become trapped in the iron in the event of a fall.

A well-fitted general-purpose saddle.

Above: Ideally there should be at least four holes for adjustment to the length of the stirrup leathers.

Stirrup irons
(left to right) regular stirrup iron; twisted (safety) iron; peacock iron.

Girths

Girths come in a variety of designs and are made of leather, a synthetic material, or 'string' (nylon). A correct-sized girth for the pony will fasten midway up the girth straps on both sides, allowing it to be tightened or loosened as necessary. A wide girth with a shaped design will spread the pressure and allow free movement of the forelegs. If the pony is prone to girth galls you can use a girth sleeve. These are often made of sheepskin and help to prevent rubbing or pinching of the skin.

Numnahs and saddle cloths

The purpose of a numnah or saddle cloth is to keep the saddle clean and to provide a *small* amount of padding between the pony and the saddle. These are not to be confused with specialist pads which are sometimes recommended by saddlers to be used in order to make the saddle fit better. A numnah should be slightly larger than the saddle and have both girth and pommel tabs to ensure it doesn't slip or wrinkle. Dirty numnahs can cause saddle rubs, so they should be washed at least once a week.

14.3 TACKING UP

Putting on a bridle

Step 1. Untie the lead rope but leave it threaded through the tying-up string.

Step 2. With the rope still untied, unbuckle the headcollar, slip it off the pony's nose and refasten around his neck.

Step 3. Standing on his left-hand side, take the bridle in your left hand and, with your right hand, place the reins over his head, taking them all the way back to his withers.

Before you tack up your pony, place your saddle and bridle out of his reach.

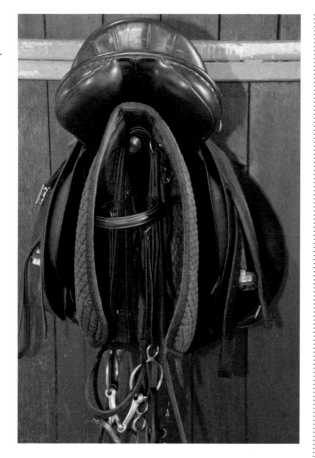

Step 4. Still with the bridle in your left hand, take your right hand under his jaw, finishing with the palm of your right hand on the front of his nose.

Step 5. Bring the bridle level with his head, then carefully transfer it into your right hand – this will leave the bit under his nose and mouth.

Step 6. Rest the bit in your left hand and raise it towards his mouth while simultaneously lifting the bridle with your right hand.

Step 7. Gently push the bit against his lips. If he does not open his mouth, push the thumb of your left hand firmly into the corner of his lip.

Step 8. Once he has opened his mouth you can raise the bridle with your right hand while guiding the bit into his mouth with your left hand.

Step 9. Place the headpiece over his right ear and then his left, taking care not to let the bit drop out of his mouth. Pull out his forelock so that it sits over the browband and any mane which may be caught under the headpiece.

Step 10. Look at the pony from the front and adjust the bridle so that it lies flat and straight before you fasten the buckles. Always put the straps in the keepers.

Top left: Untie the rope and fasten the headcollar round the pony's neck and put the reins over his head.

Top right: Place the bit under his mouth.

Below left: Use your thumb to encourage him to open his mouth.

Below right: Place the right ear through the headpiece first.

Checking the fit

First, fasten the throatlash, which should have a clearance of a hand's span (10–12cm/4–5in) between his jaw and the strap. The noseband should be secured with the buckle either at the side or directly under the jaw bone and tightened appropriately so that it fits snugly to the pony's face. It should sit approximately two finger's width (approximately 4cm/1½in) below the protruding cheekbone. If you are using a noseband that fastens below the bit, care should be taken to avoid the buckle being secured on his lip. There should be no more than a finger's width clearance between his forehead and the browband. The bit should sit at such a height as to cause two wrinkles at either side of his mouth. If the bit sits too low the pony may be able to get his tongue over it, which may cause him to panic and possibly bolt.

Top left: Fastening the throatlash.

Top centre: A well-fitted throatlash should have roughly 10cm (4in) clearance.

Top right: When fastening buckles tuck the slack into the keepers.

Lower left: The noseband should fit securely.

Lower right: A well-fitting bridle.

Putting on a saddle

Step 1. Check that the saddle area is clean.

Step 2. Before you put the saddle on, check that the stirrups are run up and the stirrup bars are in the open position (which is parallel to the ground) so that the leathers will come off if pulled firmly. Attach the girth to the right-hand side girth straps and fold it over the seat.

Step 3. Stand on the pony's left and place the numnah on his back (unless it is already attached to the saddle), slightly in front of the withers.

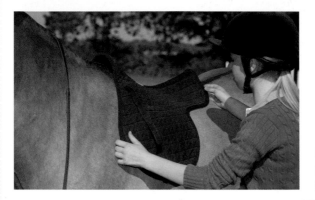

Ensure that the numnah is the correct size for the saddle.

Step 4. Place the saddle on the numnah and slide it back, following the lie of the pony's coat so that it sits just behind the pony's shoulders. Pull the numnah up into the gullet of the saddle and secure the girth strap tabs.

Step 5. Place your hand on the seat of the saddle and unfurl the girth, threading it through the tabs on the numnah and bringing it under the pony's chest to fasten. To ensure pressure is evenly spread, buckle the girth to the first and third, or first and second girth straps. If you are using a martingale remember to thread the girth through the strap before attaching it.

Step 6. Tighten the girth enough so that the saddle does not slip when your child gets on. The girth will need to be tightened further once the rider is mounted and checked again once the child has been in the saddle for a few minutes.

Top left: Lift the saddle onto the pony's back.

Top right: The numnah should fit high into the gullet of the saddle to prevent pressure points.

Bottom left: Thread the girth through the numnah straps.

Bottom right: Girth buckles should be covered with a girth guard to prevent excessive wear to the saddle.

Leaving a pony tacked up

Once the pony is tacked up you may need to leave him tied up for a short time. To do this safely, twist the reins together and thread the throatlash through the reins and fasten. Fit a headcollar over the bridle and attach the rope to a tie-up string. In cold weather place a rug over the saddle and secure both chest and belly straps.

If you are going to tie up your pony after he is tacked up, twist the reins and thread the throatlash through before fastening the headcollar over the bridle.

14.4 UNTACKING

Step 1. Fit the headcollar and rope over the bridle and tie the pony up in an appropriate area.

Step 2. 'Run up' the stirrups and unfasten the girth on his left-hand side, taking care to unthread the martingale (if you are using one) from the girth.

Step 3. Fold the girth over the seat of the saddle and remove the saddle by lifting it clear of his spine.

Step 4. To keep control of the pony, slip the headcollar around his neck and untie the rope, remembering to keep it threaded through the tying-up string.

Step 5. Unbuckle the throatlash and noseband. Standing on his left, hook your right arm under his throat and take hold of the right side of the bridle, just below his ear. Place your left hand in the same position on the left-hand side of the bridle.

Step 6. Lift the bridle off his head with an up and forward motion. This allows you to then lower the bridle slowly, giving him time to open his mouth and avoid hitting his teeth with the bit.

Step 7. Thread the bridle onto the crook of your left arm, which allows you to use both hands to refit the headcollar.

Step 8. Finally bring the reins and martingale neck strap over the pony's head and retie the rope.

14.5 CLEANING AND STORING TACK

Encourage your child to wipe their tack over with a clean, damp cloth and a small amount of saddle soap after every use. Tack that has become wet and muddy will need a more thorough clean. Once a week the tack

should be taken apart and cleaned thoroughly. Keeping the tack in good condition will ensure that the leather remains supple and strong and that any wear and tear is spotted early. Particular attention should be paid to stitching on both the bridle and the saddle to prevent it becoming a safety issue. Keeping the tack and numnahs or saddle cloths clean will reduce the risk of the pony developing any sores or discomfort.

Above left: Take the tack apart to give it a thorough clean.

Above right: Wipe the tack over with a damp sponge to remove grease before applying saddle soap.

Cleaning the bridle

Take the bridle apart and lay all the pieces on a towel or clean surface. To help you reassemble the bridle it is worth making a note of which holes your buckles are set on. Wipe over all the leather with a damp sponge to remove mud and grease. Rinse the sponge regularly and change the water at intervals to make the cleaning most effective. Having removed

Rubber reins provide a good grip and should be washed in warm soapy water.

all the dirt and grease, apply a thin layer of leather soap with a clean sponge. To keep the leather soft and supple a leather balm or conditioner can be applied with a clean, dry sponge. To clean the bit, soak it in water but do not add any detergent.

Cleaning the saddle

Remove the stirrup leathers and irons and place the irons and rubber treads in warm water to soak. Clean all the leather-work, using the same method as above. If you are using a synthetic girth clean it in warm water using a nail brush to remove dirt and grease. 'String' girths can be washed in a washing machine and hung out to dry. To add a little shine to the stirrup irons, use a metal polish. A synthetic saddle can be wiped over with a damp cloth.

Storing your tack

When storing your saddle, care needs to be taken not to damage either the tree or the weight-bearing panels. We suggest that you invest in either a saddle rack, which is fixed to a wall, or a free-standing saddle 'horse'. Place the saddle on the rack with the numnah and girth lying flat over the top. Hang your bridle from the headpiece, with the reins threaded through the throatlash. Ideally in the tack room there should be a small heater set on a timer, which will ensure that tack does not go mouldy. However, if the room is *too warm* the leather will dry out and crack.

15

Rugs and Other Equipment

There is a wide range of equipment available on the market. We outline the main types of rugs, boots and bandages and their uses. We have also included the essential safety equipment your child will require.

15.1 RUGS AND THEIR USES

How many rugs does your pony need?

The number of rugs your pony will need depends upon his type, his living conditions, his age and whether or not he is clipped. We suggest you keep the rug collection to a minimum and invest in fewer, good-quality rugs that are the correct fit for the pony.

Turnout rugs

These are intended to be worn when the pony is out at grass. They come in three weights: light, medium and heavy. They are waterproof, breathable and durable. Some come with integral neck covers while others have an attachment to which you can secure a separate neck cover. Investing in all three weights of rugs will ensure that your pony will be adequately protected, whatever the weather. These rugs can also double as stable rugs.

A turnout rug is waterproof, breathable and durable and some have either an integral neck or one that can be detached.

Turnout rugs come in three weights, light, medium and heavyweight.

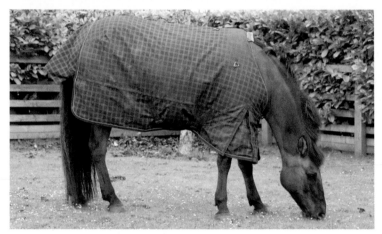

An example of a well-fitting stable rug.

Stable rugs

These are available in a number of designs and weights. They are primarily used to keep a clipped pony warm during the winter whilst stabled. They are not suitable for outdoor use.

Fly rug and mask and sweet itch rug

Made from increasingly technical fabrics, fly rugs are designed to protect the pony from insects during the summer months.

Sweet itch rugs are specifically designed to protect ponies who have developed a hypersensitivity to the biting midge. The design and effectiveness of these rugs are constantly being improved, so if your pony suffers from this allergy we suggest that you research the latest products on the market.

While some fly rugs have integral masks, separate fly masks are also available, which fasten over the pony's head and offer protection to the eyes.

Cooler rug

Different designs are available but the main purpose of the cooler rug is to wick sweat away from the coat, allowing the pony to cool down after exercise without catching a chill.

Hoods, necks and bibs

Hoods are used primarily to keep a pony's head and neck clean. They are generally made of stretchy material. Some designs will pull over the pony's head very much like a large stocking, while others will have a zip that runs from the chin to the chest.

A hood will keep your pony's head and neck clean.

Both indoor and outdoor rugs are designed either with an integral neck or with fastenings to allow a separate neck to be attached. Necks will keep the pony warmer in the winter, as well as cleaner. Be aware that necks can rub the pony's mane to the point of baldness. They fasten either with buckles or zips.

Bibs are designed to fit underneath the pony's rug and protect him from rubs to the withers and shoulders. We advise that ponies who are wearing rugs for long periods should wear bibs.

15.2 HOW TO FIT A RUG

Measuring your pony

Rugs are usually measured in feet and inches and are available in sizes that increase by increments of 3 inches. Broadly speaking the more expensive brands tend to be more versatile in their cut. To measure your pony, hold the tape measure from the point of shoulder all the way to the point of buttock. If your pony is between sizes it is advisable

Measuring the pony for a rug from point of shoulder to point of buttock.

to buy the larger size. A well-fitting rug should reach from the pony's withers to the top of his tail. When it is fastened you should be able to fit a hand sideways under it at the shoulder and where it fastens at the centre of the chest.

A well-fitting rug should sit along the line of the shoulder and the chest buckle should fasten at the base of the neck. This reduces the amount the rug rubs the shoulders. If the rug is too big for the pony he runs the risk of getting his legs caught in the straps, causing discomfort and possibly injury.

Chest fastening on a rug.

Putting on a rug

Step 1. Tie up your pony.

Step 2. Fold the rug by taking the tail end to the withers end.

Step 3. Approach the left-hand side of the pony. Lay the rug a little ahead of the pony's withers and unfold the rug over his quarters. Check that it is lying straight on his back.

Step 4. Fasten the chest buckles, gently pulling the rug back so that it fits. Never pull a rug forward as this will rub the hair the wrong way and make the pony uncomfortable.

Step 5. Secure the surcingles (the straps) which cross each other from front to back underneath his belly.

Step 6. Attach the leg straps that interlock around the hind legs. You should be able to get a hand's width between each strap and the leg. Some rug designs have a fillet string which goes underneath the tail.

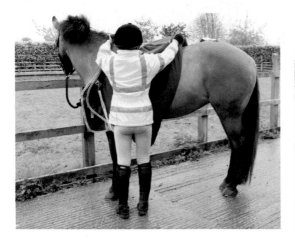

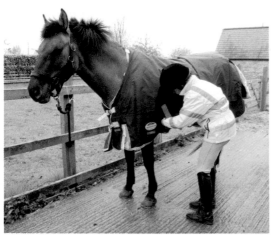
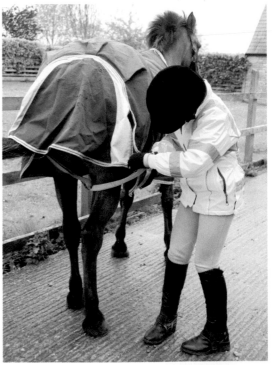

Top left: Place the rug on the pony a little ahead of his withers.

Top right: Unfold the rug over his quarters.

Above: Secure the surcingles which cross each other from front to back underneath his belly.

Right: Leg straps interlock around the hind legs.

15.3 STORING AND CLEANING RUGS

Outdoor rugs should be hung on racks so that they dry out before they are put back on the pony. A heated rug room is the perfect solution. Any rips or broken straps need to be repaired. Outdoor rugs should be cleaned and re-proofed at least once a year. Ideally use a rug laundry service. Indoor rugs should be cleaned at least once a season. Bibs and hoods can be washed in a conventional machine. Rugs that are not being used should be stored in a dry, well-ventilated, vermin-free area.

Hang up outdoor rugs so that they can dry.

15.4 BOOTS

Boots are broadly used to prevent injury and provide support. When fitting any boot (with the exception of overreach boots) the buckles or fastenings must be on the outside of the limb. When putting on the boot, slide it down the leg until it covers the relevant area. If you fasten the middle strap first this secures the boot while you do up the additional straps.

Travel boots

These are used to protect the legs when the pony is travelling. They are padded rather than rigid. The front boots are shaped to provide protection to the front of the knee while still allowing the joint to flex. Hind boots are designed to fit around the hock. Some ponies dislike wearing travel boots, particularly on their hind limbs, and this can make them unsettled and more difficult to load. If this is the case you could use travel bandages instead.

Right: A hind travel boot is designed to fit around the hock.

Far right: A front travel boot will provide protection to the front of the knee but still allows the joint to flex.

Below: Brushing boots (the higher boot shown above the fetlock) prevent injuries to the inside aspect of the lower limb caused by 'brushing' it with the opposing hoof. Overreach boots (lower) protect the heel of the forelimb from injury caused by the toe of the hind leg.

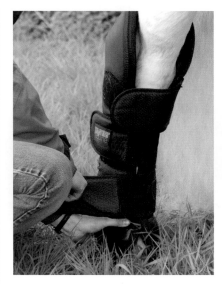

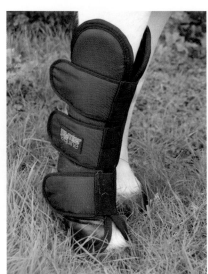

Brushing boots

These are designed to prevent the pony injuring the inside aspect of his lower limb by 'brushing' it with the opposing hoof. These are made of leather or synthetic material and have either Velcro straps or buckles to secure them onto the leg.

Overreach boots

These will minimise the risk of injury (known as an over-reach) to the heels of the forelimbs caused by the toes of the hind limbs. Shaped like a bell, these boots are designed to fit over the hoof. They are almost always made from rubber and will secure with Velcro or a buckle. A well-fitting overreach boot should touch the ground at the heel.

Tendon boots

Worn on the front limbs, the rigid shell of the boot will help protect the tendons (which run down the back of the limb) from the toes of the hind feet.

15.5 BANDAGES

Tail bandage

This is a narrow, elasticated bandage used to protect the tail when travelling and to smooth the tail after washing. This must not be left on the tail for a prolonged period, or used if the bandage is wet.

Applying a tail bandage

Step 1. Approach the pony's shoulder and run your hand down his back.

Step 2. Stand slightly off to one side.

Step 3. With the rolled bandage in your right hand unfurl 30cm (1ft) of bandage and place under the tail Take it as far up under the dock as you can and fold round the tail.

Step 4. Bandage down the tail, using even pressure and making sure the wraps overlap but are an even distance apart.

Step 5. Continue to the end of the dock and then work your way back up, finishing midway up the dock.

Step 6. Secure the bandage with the tabs, tying them in a double bow slightly to one side. Fold a layer of the bandage over the bow to keep it in place.

See the sequence of photos overleaf.

To remove the bandage, untie the tabs, gently loosen the bandage from the top using both hands – do not tug –and slip it off. (If you have bandaged over a plaited tail you will need to unroll the bandage to remove it.)

Leg bandages

These broad, inelastic cotton polyester mix bandages are designed to be used either as a stable or a travel bandage. They are secured with Velcro tabs and must always be applied over leg wraps (padding). However,

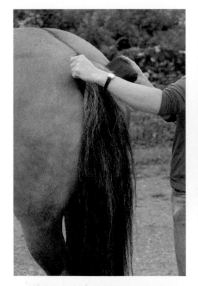
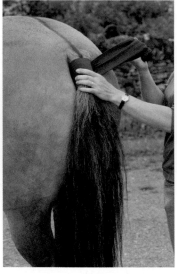
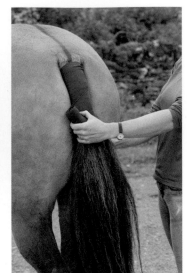

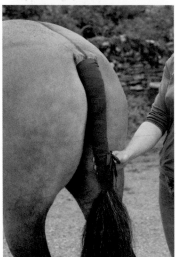

Above left: Always stand at the side of your pony to put on a tail bandage.

Above centre: Start the bandage as high up the tail as possible.

Above right: Bandage down the tail, using even pressure.

Left: Secure the finished bandage with a bow either at the front or the side of the tail.

Right: For a neat finish and to avoid the bow coming undone, fold over a wrap to cover it.

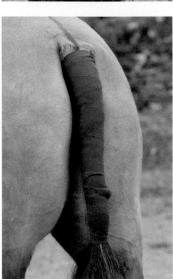

polo bandages can be used for exercise and are applied without padding. Bandages should be clean and dry before you use them.

Applying a travel bandage

Travel bandages and wraps must be correctly applied so that they provide adequate protection and support and do not unravel or cause pressure points.

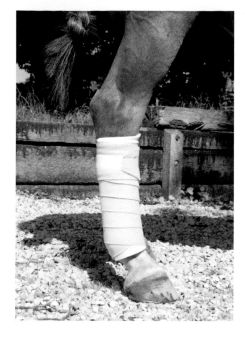

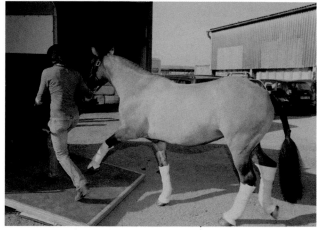

Left: Always bandage over a wrap and secure the Velcro strap on the outside of the limb.

Ready for travel, wearing travel bandages and a tail bandage.

Bandage the leg using the same techniques as you would when applying a stable bandage (see Chapter 13). Ensure that the wrap is long enough so that you can bandage over the coronary band, and the bulbs of the heel are adequately protected.

To remove a leg bandage, undo the fastening then pass the bandage from hand to hand as you unwind it.

15.6 ESSENTIAL RIDING KIT

Riding hat

Your child must have a riding hat which is of a current approved standard and has been fitted by a qualified fitter. The way the hat is stored is important if it is to remain an effective life-saving piece of equipment. Hats should ideally be kept in a hat bag and not exposed to extremes of temperature. Avoid dropping the hat or leaving it rattling around in the car as this will lead to tiny areas of damage and the hat will no longer be safe to use. If your child falls and hits their head you must replace the hat. Hats can either have a fixed peak or a skull cap design. If your child is riding cross-country the rules stipulate that skull caps with three-point harnesses must be worn.

It is a legal requirement for children under the age of 14 to wear a riding hat when riding on the road.

Do not buy a second-hand hat.

The riding hat should be of a current, approved standard and will need to be replaced if your child has a fall and hits their head.

Below: Body protectors should be professionally fitted and will need to be replaced as your child grows.

Body protector

Traditional non-inflating body protectors are mandatory for junior members of the Pony Club, anyone competing in cross-country (and often for anyone using cross-country practice facilities). If your child is competing in a specific discipline you will need to check beforehand about which model/class of protector is required. The major function is to minimise crush injuries and help protect the riders' major organs. They must be professionally fitted. As your child grows you will need to replace the body protector.

Gloves

Your child should wear gloves when handling and riding their pony. Gloves will protect their hands against rope burns and provide added grip. There is a huge variety of riding gloves on the market. Thinner gloves will provide a better 'feel' when riding but warmer, thicker gloves will be more suitable when the weather is cold.

Wearing chaps over short boots will protect your child's legs.

Boots

We strongly advise that your child only wears boots that are designed for the job. Riding boots have a pronounced heel, a relatively smooth sole and a tapered toe. All of these features provide support for the rider's foot while allowing it to be released from the stirrup in the case of a fall. Long boots or short boots worn with chaps will also protect your child's lower legs from pinching from the stirrup leathers.

Wellingtons and trainers do not have the design features associated with proper riding footwear, making them likely to jam in the stirrup iron in the case of a fall. With one foot stuck in a stirrup iron the rider is at a significant risk of being dragged and sustaining a serious injury.

16

Transport and Travelling

It is sensible to learn how to load and unload your pony safely, even if you do not have your own transport. We explain how to deal with a pony who is unwilling to load and what to do in an emergency.

16.1 TOWING AND THE LAW

Before hitching up a trailer, contact the manufacturer of your car to establish the maximum weight your vehicle can tow. By law the weight of the trailer combined with the weight of the animals must not exceed the total permitted weight.

If you hold a driving licence that was issued after January 1997 you will be required to pass the official trailer towing test in order to legally tow a pony in a trailer. We advise that you clarify current laws regarding towing on the Department of Transport website.

You are legally required to ensure that the number plate on the back of a trailer corresponds to the licence plate of the vehicle towing the trailer. It must be a road-legal licence plate (yellow).

A trailer does not require tax or an MOT but, like a lorry, should be serviced regularly.

Please note that an HGV licence will be needed if you drive a lorry over a certain weight.

By law your pony must travel with his passport.

16.2 SAFETY CHECKS

If your trailer or lorry has been off the road for a prolonged period then it is always advisable to have it serviced.

Before you set out on your journey you need to pay close attention to the general condition of your trailer/lorry. First, ensure the tyre pressure is in line with manufacturer's guidelines. Spend time checking that all lights are in working order. In the case of a trailer the jockey wheel must be in working order. It must be able not only to be wound down but also to be secured in the wound up position. The emergency brake – which usually takes the form of high-tensile wire – connects the trailer to the vehicle by means of a loop over the tow hitch. The function of the brake is to stop the trailer if it becomes detached from the towing vehicle when in use. Ensure that the ramps can be opened and closed and that they fasten securely. If you are travelling your pony with a partition it must be securely fastened in line with manufacturer's guidelines. This is also the case with breast and breech bars. Often trailers will have small skylights for ventilation: these must open and close. You will not be able to assess the state of the floor reliably, which is why we recommend regular services.

16.3 PREPARING TO MOVE

Checklist

Pack your vehicle with everything you need for the trip before you load the pony. Compile a checklist so you do not forget any important equipment:

- Tack – including girth and numnah and a spare headcollar and rope.

- Water buckets and filled water carriers.

- Haynet.

- Appropriate rugs.

- First aid kits (human and equine).

- Grooming kit and extra hoof pick.

- Hat, body protector, medical armband (required for cross-country events), gloves, boots, whip.

What the pony wears

To travel your pony safely he will require a well-fitting leather head-collar and a lead rope that is in good condition. Fit either travel boots or travel bandages with wraps (see Chapter 15). His tail should be protected from rubbing on the bar or back ramp with either a tail bandage (see Chapter 15) or a tail guard. Depending on the weather conditions,

Below left: Tail bandage with tail guard over the top.

Below right: Ready for travel wearing a tail bandage, travel boots, a cotton sheet and a leather headcollar with lead rope.

whether or not he is clipped and how comfortable he is travelling will determine whether he wears a rug. Whatever rug you put on him must fit securely. It is advisable to take a rug with you even if he is not travelling in one.

16.4 LOADING AND UNLOADING

Before you load the pony we advise you to park your trailer/lorry in a relatively secure area so that there is no danger of the pony getting loose on to a road. Ideally you will park so that you are facing the direction you are planning to go. Let down the ramp and open partitions, front doors or flaps. This will make the vehicle appear more inviting to the pony and allow the handler to get out easily once the pony is loaded.

Always wear gloves and sturdy footwear when loading or unloading a pony. Remember that if you remain calm and positive the pony is more likely to load first time. Stand on the pony's left side and walk him to the trailer ramp, making sure that he is as straight as possible. Walk a little ahead of his shoulder (but do not get in front of him) and

The partition should be fastened back before you load the pony.

walk purposefully up the ramp, allowing him enough space. Once you are in the vehicle, tie him to string and secure the partition and breech bar before closing the ramp. Exit via the jockey door, remembering to secure it behind you.

If your pony is travelling by himself in a trailer you should load him on the right side to allow better stability when travelling.

When you come to unload the pony you should park the vehicle where there is sufficient space around you so that he can walk out safely. First, lower the front ramp (where applicable). Go to the pony and untie the rope before you release the breast bar/partition. Walk the pony down the ramp, allowing him enough room. In the absence of a front ramp you will have to 'back' the pony out of the trailer. In this instance you will need help to lower the breech bar while you untie the pony.

Above: Lead the pony up the ramp, making sure he is as straight as possible.

Right: Once the pony is in the trailer, secure the partition and breech bar immediately.

A pony who is difficult to load

Some ponies may be apprehensive about loading. There are several techniques that can help.

- Some ponies are happier to travel if they have a companion on board.

- Use a bridle over the top of his headcollar to give you more control, and a lunge line to provide additional length and safety.

- A useful technique is to attach lunge lines on either side of the vehicle. You will need two people to hold the lines and, when the pony is presented to the ramp, cross the lines behind the pony and gently apply pressure to his quarters. The assistants (who should also wear safety hats and gloves) must stand at a safe distance to avoid being kicked or trampled.

- You *can* use food to encourage your pony to load, but we do not recommend it as some ponies will become cantankerous and unruly when food is in the equation.

Using a bridle (without the noseband and reins) over a headcollar will provide you with more control. Clip the rope onto a Newmarket chain, which is attached to the bit rings.

Lunge lines can be helpful to keep the pony straight and encourage him to go forwards into the trailer.

16.5 IN THE CASE OF EMERGENCIES

Remaining calm will help you deal with any emergency more effectively. We advise that you have specific breakdown cover designed for transporting horses/ponies.

If the vehicle has either broken down or cannot be mended at the roadside you will have to move your pony to alternative transport. We strongly advise that, if possible, you find an off-road area to unload the pony. In the case of you breaking down on a motorway you must remain in the vehicle. Call your breakdown cover and await police assistance. Livestock on the motorway is a significant risk to public safety.

Do not unload your pony on a major road unless emergency staff recommend this and assist with traffic management. Ponies are always safer in the trailer/lorry.

In the case of an injured or distressed pony you must never get into the trailer or lorry with him. You will need a vet and possibly the emergency services in order that the situation can be dealt with safely.

17

Tuition

A key factor in helping your child build a rewarding and successful partnership with their pony and overcome any problems is for them to have lessons with a qualified instructor. In addition, enrolling your child in their local branch of the Pony Club will give them the chance to benefit from a greater variety of tuition and encourage them to thrive in a fun and social learning environment.

17.1 WHAT'S IN A NAME?

There are a number of qualifications that entitle people to teach and the most widely respected are those endorsed by the British Horse Society (BHS). In addition, there are a number of discipline-specific bodies that have their own teaching qualifications. Generally speaking it is advisable to look for an instructor who has a background in teaching children and holds some level of qualification. The BHSPTT (preliminary teaching test) is the first rung on the teaching ladder. This is followed by the BHSAI (assistant instructor), the BHSII (intermediate instructor) and the BHSI (instructor). Another available qualification

A child's confidence will increase with regular tuition.

Rosettes may be the outcome of a successful partnership.

is the UKCC (UK Coaching Certificate) which award levels 1,2 and 3 in sports coaching. The UKCC level 2 is broadly equivalent to the BHSPTT.

17.2 CHOOSING AN INSTRUCTOR

If your child is currently having lessons at a riding school you may find that continuing to take advantage of its facilities and trainers is the best way forward. Another option is to employ the services of an independent instructor. This will give your child a greater degree of continuity in teaching methods and a more personal approach to their lessons. The BHS holds an up-to-date register of freelance instructors and approved training establishments. If your child is the member of the Pony Club you can ask the District Commissioner of your local branch for the names of instructors used by the Club. Whoever you employ to teach your child should demonstrate a sensible approach to safety and hold a current and relevant first aid certificate along with appropriate

Joining a branch of the Pony Club is a great way for your child to have fun and improve their skills.

The British Horse Society has an up-to-date register of freelance instructors and approved riding establishments.

insurance documents and a child protection and safeguarding certificate. The BHS register also endorses continuous regular training of instructors, all the relevant insurances as well as DBS (criminal record) checks.

17.3 ASSESSING A LESSON

In order for your child to improve their riding skills it is essential that confidence and enjoyment are part of their learning experience. We explain how to assess a riding lesson so that you are able to judge for yourself whether you have chosen the right instructor for your child and their pony. Young or novice riders tend to benefit from sessions of about 30 minutes.

Lesson content

- Core skills – young and novice riders will benefit most from attention paid to improving their basic position and skills such as balance, transitions and steering.

- Relevance – an accomplished instructor will outline the practical reasons for the techniques and approaches which they are using.

- Instilling confidence – with a new rider/pony combination it is important to work on confidence and familiarity as these aspects are key if the partnership is to progress.

- Enjoyment – if your child is to maintain their enthusiasm and motivation to learn, the lessons must be fun.

- Progression – in order to ensure continued development of the rider's abilities and techniques there should be an emphasis on increasing their knowledge and understanding.

Some ponies may need a bit of encouragement to jump a fence.

Teaching style

If the teaching is to be effective, communication is the key. An interactive and approachable delivery style will ensure the lesson is constructive. Look for the following.

- Empathy and rapport – a good instructor will be enthusiastic and have empathy for their pupil. They will be able to encourage and motivate without pressurising the situation.

- Professionalism – while the instructor needs to be liked by the child they need to maintain authority and control over the sessions to keep the lessons focused and structured.

- Continuity – a consistent approach with regard to technique, focus and priorities is essential if the child is to develop and progress.

- Compatibility – this component is relevant on two levels; the instructor you have chosen must have a teaching style that your child responds to, and also an understanding of the level they are being asked to teach at, so that their plans for your child's progress match your own.

- Flexibility – a confident and competent instructor will have the ability to adapt both their lesson plan and their approach to suit the child in front of them. The positive outcome of this is that goals can be both set and achieved within a reasonable time frame.

A good instructor will be able to adapt their approach to suit the individual child and pony.

Index